BEYOND LIMITS

Carmelo Rodríguez

Beyond Limits

Copyright © 2025 by Carmelo Rodriguez

ALL RIGHTS RESERVED

This book is intended for informational and inspirational purposes only. It is not a substitute for professional medical advice, diagnosis, therapy, or treatment. The author is not a licensed mental health professional, and the content provided should not be used as a replacement for advice from qualified healthcare providers, including licensed counselors, psychologists, or physicians. Always seek the guidance of a licensed professional or healthcare provider with any questions you may have regarding your mental health or a medical condition. Never disregard professional advice or delay seeking it because of something you have read in this book. If you are experiencing a mental health crisis or are in danger, please contact emergency services or a mental health crisis line in your area immediately. The reader assumes full responsibility for how they choose to use this information. The author and publisher disclaim any liability arising directly or indirectly from the use or misuse of the information contained in this book.

Publisher: Absolute Author Publishing House
Editor: Dr. Melissa Caudle
Associate Editor: Kathy Kittok

Paperback ISBN: 979-8-89401-079-3
eBook ISBN: 979-8-89401-080-9

PRINTED IN THE UNITED STATES OF AMERICA

TABLE OF CONTENTS

Foreword i

Introduction v

Chapter One 1

Chapter Two 9

Chapter Three 23

Chapter Four 38

Chapter Five 49

Chapter Six 63

Chapter Seven 76

Chapter Eight 87

Chapter Nine 100

Chapter Ten 112

Chapter Eleven 125

Chapter Twelve 139

Chapter Thirteen 148

Chapter Fourteen 162

Chapter Fifteen 173

Chapter Sixteen 183

Chapter Seventeen 190

About the Author 197

Foreword

By Dr. Melissa Caudle

When I first opened this manuscript, I had just begun my battle—one I never saw coming. Following spinal surgery on April 10, 2025, where I had to have cages, rods, and screws at my L2-L4, I woke up paralyzed on my left side. It was supposed to be a three-day hospital stay, but it turned out to be over a month. My leg was lifeless, and I couldn't feel anything at all. My foot was numb, too. The pain and the electrical shocks shooting down my leg were unbearable. However, what tore at me most was the uncertainty: *Would I ever walk again?* Would I reclaim the life I'd worked so hard to build?

Doctors told me the recovery could take two years, if at all, depending on the amount of nerve damage, and I would be a wheelchair user or use an electric mobility scooter for years. "But, there is a chance your nerves will heal depending on the amount of nerve damage," my surgeon said, trying to reassure me or stop me from crying. Some days, those words sounded like hope. Other days, they felt like a life sentence as I am currently in home health care and home physical therapy, trying to learn to walk with braces on my ankle and my thigh down to my mid-calf to help steady me. I have to wear them to support my left side, which is painful. Every step I failed to take was gut-wrenching. I began to feel like a burden to my husband and my daughter, who moved back in with us to help me.

That's when I read and edited *Beyond Limits*. I've edited many of Carmelo's books in the last five years, but this one hit me at my core and seemed personal to me. His words touched me and encouraged me. Now, with assistance, using a walker and physical support from my husband, I can "walk" from my bedroom to my living room. It takes about ten minutes, but it is progress. Every time I lose hope or feel tears, I remember the encouragement in *Beyond Limits*.

This book isn't just a memoir of trauma—it's a lifeline. A raw, unfiltered narrative of a man who defied death, not once, but time and again. It's the account of a soul

BEYOND LIMITS

flung into darkness, clawing his way back—broken bones, shattered dreams, and all. It's a mirror for anyone who's ever questioned whether they can survive or do the unthinkable. For me, my unthinkable is to walk again. What's yours?

For those of us staring down a long road of recovery…

For the ones who've felt the sting of depression, panic attacks, or the ghost of suicidal thoughts…

For anyone who's cried in silence and needs the courage to fight…

This book is for *you*.

Through every page, I felt seen not only as a patient facing a long-term recovery but also as a person, a fighter. If I learned one thing from this book and Carmelo, it is that healing isn't linear; it's a battlefield where your scars are your armor. *Beyond Limits* reminds us that trauma doesn't end us—it transforms us. So, whether you're recovering from surgery, grief, abuse, or invisible battles no one else sees, know this: there is power in your pain, and on the hardest days,

Carmelo Rodriguez

let this book be your companion. Let it remind you, like it reminded me, that you're not alone—and you're not done yet.

You're still here, and that means your story isn't over; a new chapter in your life begins.

Best regards,

Dr. Melissa Caudle
Bestselling Author, Survivor, and Advocate for Hope

Introduction

Every breath, heavy and labored, fights against the suffocating grip of fate. Each inhale feels like sandpaper scraping against the walls of my windpipe. Moving air in and out of my lungs quickly becomes an arduous chore, a labor every fiber of my physical being is resisting. The sky looms above, a dull expanse of gray devoid of any inspiration, and even if I couldn't see it clearly through some shattered glass of a helmet and not the film of tears and blood clouding my vision, it wouldn't evoke any sense of poetry.

Here I lie, sprawled upon the unforgiving earth, covered in dirt after being brought to an abrupt halt by the cruel hand of Kismet. In this moment, faced with the daunting task of simply surviving, I realize it is a challenge far greater than any task I've dared or any adventure I've embarked upon in my decades of existence.

It stands as the pinnacle of all endeavors, a task so monumental that it dwarfs the grandest feats of existence. Grounded and helpless, I'm thrust into the greatest battle I have ever been in,

Carmelo Rodriguez

and the prize is measly. As invaluable as immaterial as one more breath.

The world spun horrifyingly countless times in the moments before this, and by many accounts, I have found my way to death's very door. The grim reaper lingers with a hand on my shoulder, and I feel its touch with my chest slowly caving in and my heart beating towards oblivion. Yet at this moment, hoisted by the petard of my virtues and desire, as my body inches closer to a surrender, quick to become one with the dirt on which I lay, the voice in my head sweeps past the numbing pain to keep the very last fibers of muscles of breathing in my body working for my life's greatest challenge.

To live.

"I think there was a bit of confusion. I'm not a veterinarian; I've never been. I am a military combat veteran."

These words, a response clarifying a misunderstanding yet subtly reflecting my seasoned experience, carried a weight I hadn't really expected would be such a privilege to voice again. I had never been one to take life for granted, regardless of my adventures or my undertakings. But fate doesn't discriminate enough to pay attention only to those who know the value of what they have, and I would learn that in the hardest way humanly possible.

From my earliest memories, the witchery of motorcycles has woven itself into the fabric of my being. Since childhood, the

BEYOND LIMITS

revving of engines and the sleek lines of bikes have stirred a deep and undying passion within me. This fascination that was born in my youth has grown over the years, shaping me into the man I would become and igniting a lifelong love affair with two-wheeled machines.

I must say that I did not fall so effortlessly in love with the world of motorcycles and riding. I had some help as soon as I realized they piqued my interest. The "effort" came from one of my favorite uncles, who was an advocate for riding and had a similar affection for motorbikes. Whether I inherited the perk from him is a debate that will probably never have a right answer.

With his inspiration, when I came of age, I indulged a curiosity I'd been harboring with my growing interest in motorcycles. I ventured into the idea of taking apart a bike to see the bits and pieces and then piecing those bits back together to see how they worked. It had often seemed like a long shot, but with each passing day, the thought morphed into a possibility in my head, and my confidence grew.

When I clocked twenty, I seized the chance to become a motorcycle owner, buying my first bike. It was, in every sense, a dream come true. From that moment on, I rode my bike at every single chance I got, and every moment, even with the happenstances of fate, was memorable.

I consider passion a privilege as it stirs, along with love and family, the desire to persevere. The passions that are the winds to my

Carmelo Rodriguez

sails are my current career in law enforcement in the heart of Washington, DC, and my writing, both of which stand as the pillars of my existence. I have a keen interest in films and the creation of a perfect cinematic experience from quality writing. Let me not forget to mention that I'm passionate about motorcycles and that the mere sight of a good one is as good to me as a breath of fresh air to my soul.

Yet amidst these passions that shape the trajectory of my life, none holds a dearer place, nor is it a greater significance than my unwavering devotion to my family. They are the compass guiding me through life's tumultuous waters, grounding me in moments of uncertainty and filling my heart with boundless love, purpose, and, ultimately, the will to survive.

There's imperfection to living, and it is called by many names, one of which is fate. Some kinks alter the paths we take as mortal beings. Sometimes, we do not realize how much we have lived or how invaluable an extra breath is to keep us going, not until we come close enough to being ushered by death, moments away from never suffering, never seeing, never feeling, never experiencing anything ever again.

Few get the chance to say that they pull one over on death, seeing as we are dying from the very moment we are born. But on the chance that such an experience comes, it forces one to dig into the deepest cores of their soul for everything from fear of the end

BEYOND LIMITS

to a reason to hold on to every breath, no matter how harrowing it feels, and everything in between.

Sometimes, the in-betweens are the ones we consider plenty consequential, but life sure is nothing without the memories we make, no matter how seemingly insignificant. Because when you have to crawl on the uneven earth, mud and dirt being the least of your worries as your inch agonizingly towards any form of intervention after life thrusts you into the air with your mean machine, a Harley Davidson, 107 Fat Boy, and sends you hurtling into the woods where you break just about everything, what helps you cling on to the breaths are the memories and the passions that made them.

BEYOND LIMITS

Chapter One

A loud ringing in my ears forces my eyes to snap open. In these first moments, my body remains oblivious to any impending surge of pain. I blink quickly and then slowly, acknowledging my return to consciousness. With a gentle sweep of my gaze, I take in the unfamiliar surroundings. I find myself barely prone, and as I tilt my head, I'm met with the sight of tall trees towering and enclosing me—the unmistakable embrace of the woods. My memory holds fragments, refusing me the luxury of what has transpired. All I can do is remind myself to keep breathing.

Each push of air out of my lungs is a basic testament to my determination to endure.

Pain is important. It is easier said than understood. I feel next to nothing in my first grasp of consciousness, and it doesn't seem at all like an illusion at this moment. The harsh breaths I've had to draw to keep myself alive count, and it seems like that is the only struggle. As I shift my gaze, the towering presence of the large tree behind me comes into view, standing as a silent witness to the enigma of my circumstances. My stare at the tree propels a temporary wonder about the role it played in my landing at its feet. Was it the one on the receiving end of my launch from my bike?

The question crosses my mind, along with the realization of the confined space around my head that's coming from the helmet I have on. Unaware of anything beyond the fact that I've been harshly disposed of, I try to summon all my strength to get on my feet, and it strikes me I can't move the rest of my body.

My paralysis sends my heart cascading inside my chest in an instant. I let moments pass before I attempt to move again. Figuring I can't pull myself up, I move my arms, and only one responds. I'm not beaten by the grasp that my other limb is immobile; it's enough for me to repeat the countless survival drills in combat situations instilled in me by the military.

A pause hits my effort, and the world spins again in an instant, and another wave of unconsciousness nears me.

I blink, and though I'm still horizontal, a light source ahead of me has become a target.

Turning is laborious, but I manage to. The ringing in my ears has dulled, and my vision is still partly misty, but I try to reorient myself, sinking into the mud to pull myself erect. As my feet contact the ground and bear the weight of my body, a new wave of reality

BEYOND LIMITS

crashes over me. Before I can even take a step, the odd angle of my stance sends a sharp surge of pain radiating through my lower limb. With trepidation, I lower my gaze to discover the grim truth: my foot is broken. I'm a mere gust of wind away from toppling back into the dirt.

***

I believe that there are two kinds of people: the hack people who are born knowing what they're meant to do with their lives, and the ones who spend however long it takes trying to figure it out. I wasn't born and hack: I had interests and passions like everyone else; I had things I did that kept me on the path to fulfilling whatever potential I had, but I wasn't dead sure about the notion of what my life was supposed to be, only what it wasn't meant to be.

Life dealt me a series of unfavorable cards. I floated around like a dandelion in the whirlwind, searching for solace and direction amidst the chaos until I found a place where it seemed like I could get myself some answers. While some turn to faith and religion, my gaze fixated on the red, white, and blue of the American flag, steadfast in front of the recruitment office of the US Army.

Unlike some who might have envisioned serving their country before they knew how to pay taxes, enlisting in the military wasn't a childhood dream or a career aspiration for me. It was a pivotal decision aimed at re-coursing the trajectory of my life. I'd gone into the office with questions in my head, but the one I was asked in a conversation with the recruiter, who asked why I wanted to join the US Army, was perhaps the most important of the entire encounter.

"I don't wanna die here. I know I have more to offer. I just haven't found it yet," was the response that I gave. I didn't know how much this statement epitomized my desperation and longing for a purposeful existence. Still, it certainly was the beginning of a lot of things, and it propelled me towards a path of self-discovery.

I was confident in my potential, yet I'll admit uncertainty clouded my vision regarding what I was truly capable of and how far I could go. Honesty compels me to admit that I couldn't foresee the ultimate destination of my path. Nonetheless, armed with unwavering tenacity, I forged ahead. Even in moments when the road ahead seemed obscured, I trusted in the power of perseverance to tilt the odds in my favor, to guide me through the unknown toward unforeseen accomplishments.

Joining the military was far from a cakewalk. Still, every time I recall walking into that recruitment center, it stands out as one of the most fundamental and ultimately life-changing decisions I have ever made for more reasons than I could count.

Perhaps a cliché about war is how much it changes one, and that was certainly true for me. Despite the grueling realities that I faced during the war I fought in my deployment, I returned home fundamentally altered. I wouldn't dare to claim that my experience in battle outscored any of the men or women who served with me, but each to his own. I felt the center of gravity within me shift from its axis by an inch.

Upon my return, while navigating the challenges of readjustment, I crafted a blueprint for my future. Life would not be the way I'd left it before I went to war, and I had to get used to it. Though the journey was laden with difficulties, I held on to the same steadfastness that had made something of me in the military, someone worth the service for his country, in my determination to carve out a meaningful life beyond the battlefield.

Life after the military, before I realized the blueprint and the tactics for my approach, had a plethora of questions about what to do with the time I now had in my hands, and amidst my plethora of thoughts came the idea of college. I spent roughly two years in college. Initially, as I was unsure which would be the best fit for me, I tested out studying various career paths. College was the junction where multiple roads led in different directions, and even though it took me a bit of time, I finally realized which of the paths felt most right.

I wouldn't deny that my military background ultimately influenced my decision, but choosing law enforcement was like putting on a glove that fit.

My first point of call in my law enforcing career was the federal prison system, where I had the role of correctional officer. My experience in the prison system taught me many things about life, and working as a correctional officer in a federal penitentiary showed me a different side to the fickleness of life. It brought along with it the understanding of the most crucial skill ins law enforcement, like being able to manage the ego, adrenaline, and testosterone of men whose default settings often were violence and chaos.

I left the prison system with a wealth of experience as I moved to Washington, DC, to continue my career in law enforcement. In the prime of my career in Washington, I got the "sting."

I've always been a fan of writing and good literature. Though I never pursued a career, the thought crossed my mind fleetingly, but I often believed that writing was more of a hobby than a career path I was going to depend fully on. In Washington, however, writing and film piqued my interest so much that I imagined the possibilities of Hollywood. It seemed at first like a far reach, but I would be tenacious with my interests. The idea of having a film credited as my work became an adventure for me to pursue, and I did.

But in the face of exploring a new hobby and adventure, there was one constant in my life, a passion that had been there for as long as I could remember. Motorcycle riding has always been an adrenaline rush for me, and regardless of time and fate, I don't think there will ever be a replacement for the thrill and the high of riding a two-wheeled machine on the road.

I fondly recall countless nights spent tearing through city streets and racing tracks, pushing the boundaries of speed and skill, even

BEYOND LIMITS

popping my first wheelie with a rush of exhilaration. It's a memory that is right there at the top of my head, one I don't think time will take away from me. Over the years, my passion for motorcycles has led me to own a diverse array of bikes, from racing motorcycles to project bikes and cruising machines.

My journey began with a CBR 600, an elegant sports bike, then progressed to a stunning Ninja 250—a project bike that helped me own my stunt skills. Venturing further, I embraced the power of a Z100 with its stiff chassis and embarked on my first experimental project: transforming a cruiser into a sleek, fully functional bobber. Stripping it down to its bare parts as I'd now mastered, I meticulously reconstructed the engine and changed every detail I could to perfection.

After countless years of exhilarating rides on and off the tracks with my Z100, I made the bittersweet decision to part ways with it and redirect my focus toward advancing my career elsewhere. Closing that chapter in my life didn't diminish my passion for motorcycles because being out of sight isn't out of mind. My hiatus fueled my curiosity to explore new horizons, and it was just like I had never left when I resumed.

Driven by a desire to test my skills and abilities, I embarked on the ambitious journey of building a bike from scratch. As each piece fell into place and the project neared completion, I had a renewed flame for motorcycle riding ignited within me, beckoning me back to the vast open road.

Carmelo Rodriguez

I had renewed determination, and I would not waste it. With it, I took the plunge and purchased my first Harley-Davidson, a milestone that marked the beginning of an unbreakable bond. Since that moment, the roar of the engine and the wind in my face have become constants, guiding me on endless adventures with unwavering joy and passion.

Now and then, when I think back to that bike and the day I bought it, a thought crosses through my mind about what I would have done had I had fate whisper to me that the Fat Boy would be the one too much. Would I have listened or missed the chance to own or ride the incredible piece of machinery? Or would I have defied fate for the thrill?

Chapter Two

You could spend your entire life storm-chasing and never see the gale till you're in the heart of it. I'm not one for religion, but I'm not oblivious to the various deities people worship, hoping to influence fate. Whether it's stone, fire, water, or even the very air we breathe, every rider is, in a way, a devotee—perhaps not fervently, but seeking a bargain nonetheless with the wind, akin to a god. It matters most to us, and we hope it will show mercy and allow us safe passage. And deep down, we want to believe that our non-prayers are heard.

When the wind is kind, it embodies the essence of thrill. There are very few experiences in life that compare to the sensation of the wind against your face as you tear down a path. It whispers promises of freedom while threatening to hold you back and yet secretly propelling the desire to push further, just one more inch.

After the very first try, you're bound to be almost tempted, you see. Even on the clearest, sunniest days, the wind answers when you call for it. But when you're on a two-wheel vehicle, the wind is never on your side. And there are moments when no offering is enough to appease its unpredictable nature. After years of riding through different seasons and weather, I wasn't unfamiliar with this sensation. There sure were moments, albeit few, when I questioned why I was on my bike when I could have been anywhere else that would have been "safer."

As I thundered down the I-95, the gusts of the heavy crosswind battered against me with wild, unyielding fury. It hadn't been that way when I first mounted the bike and began this trip. I hadn't sensed any impending storm to add to what should have been an ordinary ride. Yet, right in the middle of the highway, there was a slow, persistent knocking that I couldn't shake—it was the wind threatening to send me careening off course at any moment.

With each blast, I felt as if I was locked in a relentless battle for control of the Harley. My grip on the handlebars was white-knuckled beneath my gloves as I fought to stay upright and on track.

In a desperate bid to catch a break from the wild wind, I made a split-second decision to veer into the far-right lane on the back of years of experience. No matter the course, it was better managed when one wasn't caught between the storm and some other road user. Riding the flank on a highway was not always the greatest decision, and I soon as I did, a sense of unease prickled at the back of my neck. But I was no stranger to it. Every time I straddled my bike and hit the open road in pursuit of the thrill, I confronted the fear of the unknown head-on. And each time I emerged victorious, I never let the uncertainty that lurked around every bend get to me. It was always one or the other; you see—the thrill or the fear—each vying for dominance every time I raced down the highway, my heart pounding in sync with the roar of the engine. Still, for as long as I could remember, the thrill had always been the one fuelling my adventures, my passion for the open road.

I was hardly fazed, but little did I know that my decision would hurl me into a scramble of danger and uncertainty, hurtling me toward a fate I had never expected.

Suddenly, I was jolted from behind by a bump to my rear tire, sending a shiver down my spine. I instinctively glanced in the rear-view mirror, only to see another vehicle dangerously close, pressed against my tail. My heart lurched in my chest; an icy wave of panic crashed over me as I grasped the gravity of the situation I found myself in. Dread tightened its grip around my throat harder than I did on the handlebars of the Harley and instantly choked me with fear and uncertainty.

Without hesitation, I revved the engine again, hoping to put some distance between my bike and the vehicle behind me. That moment was as far as the clarity would afford me. That split second, when I succumbed to the panic and heeded instinct, was as far as I would go before consciousness tore away from me, and everything would change. In the next instant, a deafening crash filled the air as another vehicle collided with mine, sending me careening out of control.

Being struck was all that memory chanced me—the who and the why did not even exist at the moment when everything turned on its head. The world seemed to blur as my bike spun across the lanes of the highway, the screech of tires and the roar of the engine drowning out all other sounds. I was weightless, literally and figuratively, tossed in the air, an object at the mercy of the wind, and a prayer for gravity as I was winged over the four lanes on the highway. The fraction of a second suspended me in a terrifying moment of chaos, with my bike tossed like nothing by the force of the impact.

Then, darkness.

***

In the nation's heart's capital, amidst the towering monuments and bustling streets of Washington, D.C., I found myself on the front lines of chaos as a member of the riot squad. With the dawn of each new day, amidst the plethora of possibilities, was that of a city succumbing to agitation, frustration, or the belief in the misrepresentation of an idea, either at the government or simply at every other person. When challenges and unrest festered from protests and demonstrations, there was a time when that was where I was likely to be found.

BEYOND LIMITS

From the steps of the Capitol to the streets of Georgetown, I stood shoulder to shoulder with fellow officers, prepared to confront whatever challenges lay ahead. Our days were filled with tension, uncertainty hanging heavy in the air as we braced ourselves for the unknown, from being a human shield to bringing aggressors back down to earth.

The riot squad was a brotherhood forged in the vessel of adversity. Each lone warrior was bound by a shared sense of duty and a commitment to upholding the city's peace. Each time we trained, it was relentless, like every group that wanted to deliver when the time came. We honed our skills in crowd control, de-escalation, and conflict resolution, preparing ourselves for the trials that soon enough awaited us on the streets.

But, the hard truth was sometimes, just like in life, the scenarios we painted in preparedness do not always prove effective when the shit hits the fan. Like a game plan for a matchday when you think you know the opposition well enough because those from whose hands we tried to rip the mantles of chaos were humans, there was always the factor of unpredictability, that one soul who was going to end up either inciting the crowd or making the singular decision that caused everyone to suffer. The likes of adrenaline junkies who sought to be heroes, those who saw anyone in uniform as a dominating authority with the goal of enslaving them and would only revolt in their veins.

Carmelo Rodriguez

It made it so that we were almost never fully prepared enough of us for the sheer scale of the chaos that unfolded before our eyes. When tensions boiled over, and emotions ran high, many others and I were thrust into the midst of violent clashes and heated confrontations.

I won't deny that, amidst the chaos and turmoil, there were moments of unity and solidarity that sometimes shone through the darkness. In the heat of the fray, strangers seldom became allies, and sometimes those you feared the worst from proved to be the beacon of calm. Again, it is hard to say that there's ever a scenario best to describe the unpredictability of humans like the heart of a riot—the very eye of the storm.

Having been to war where the worst of humanity was portrayed, I was familiar with the heat of a tempest. To be on home soil, deployed to calm a city from being torn apart by strife, was not quite the same thing as facing insurgents and enemy combatants. Still, I did witness the best and worst of humanity, grappling with the complexities of justice and freedom. In many ways, being in the riot squad mirrored the journey of surviving life's challenges; the chaos and the unrest I and others faced every day were perhaps no more than the trials many people endured. I would have thought that perhaps I had received my fair share of life's whiplash if only I knew for sure what awaited me.

Before my life was heavily punctuated by the accident, and I was tossed like a rag doll along with the object of my adventure over lanes of asphalt and cast into the woods, I was fulfilling my polymathic dreams.

I was on the journey of creating my web series, "Haunted or Not," where I aimed to delve into the age-old question of actual paranormal activity versus commercial marketing scheme. The show was going to uncover the truth behind purportedly haunted locations, exploring whether their eerie reputation was genuine or merely a ploy to draw in curious tourists visiting the countless destinations that existed across the country.

With each episode, "Haunted or Not" takes viewers on a thrilling journey, investigating famous landmarks, abandoned buildings, and rumored ghostly hotspots. Armed with skepticism and a keen eye for detail, our team of intrepid investigators digs into the history and lore surrounding each address, separating fact from fiction in a quest for truth.

The idea behind "Haunted or Not" was to provide a fresh perspective on the world of paranormal investigation. I wanted to challenge preconceived notions and debunk myths along the way. Rather than sensationalizing supernatural phenomena, the approach would be grounded in critical thinking and scientific inquiry, allowing viewers to explore the unknown from a rather more critical perspective.

Each episode followed a similar format, with our team conducting thorough research, interviewing eyewitnesses, and gathering evidence. From haunted houses to purportedly cursed objects, no stone would be left unturned, even if it was possessed.

But the real magic of "Haunted or Not" lay in its ability to spark conversation and debate. By presenting both sides of the argument, we hoped to engage viewers in a dialogue about the nature of belief and skepticism using the power of storytelling, which, I would admit, I had a great interest in.

With "Haunted or Not," the line between fact and fiction would blur, leaving viewers to question what they thought they knew about the supernatural.

Back to the art of storytelling, I leveraged my extensive experience as a former correctional officer within the federal prison system to add authenticity to my writing. Fully conscious of the complex dynamics of prison life, I embarked on creating a trilogy of novels set within the confines of these institutions, and though I'd had books I'd written prior to this, the undoing project took a turn I didn't quite envisage, considering how raw it came out, from the first book of the series to the last, the story very much took a life of its own, that even I, as the writer, became a mere spectator to the insanity of the semi-fictional characters.

I might be biased to say that this trilogy is one of the best works of my creativity, even as I was stripped of a chance to keep the rhythm of the project with my writing following my abrupt slinging from my bike on the I-95.

BEYOND LIMITS

Aside from the trilogy, which was yet to see the light of day, the very last book project I worked on, "Smile," before an ultimate timeout, turned out to be a bestseller. After pouring my heart and soul into every endeavor, driven by a steadfast belief in giving my all because whatever was worth doing in the first place was worth doing well, I barely had a moment to revel in the glory of becoming a bestselling author. Like a phoenix rising from the ashes, I had only just begun to spread my wings when fate tore me down, casting me into the depths of the woods by the roadside of the highway.

My journey as a spectator didn't end with my book; another facet of my writing was unfolding in the glitz and glamour of Las Vegas, where my work was being transformed into a film. This was the culmination of years of dreaming and striving, the realization of a fantasy I long held dear, working with a renowned director and witnessing my words come to life on the grand stage of the silver screen.

Another exciting opportunity that awaited me in Hollywood was a prominent podcast, *The Real American Cholo Podcast*, which I'd recently finished; it was one with a vast audience that was bound to amplify my presence and deepen my ties within the industry. This platform promised to catapult my name into the spotlight and solidify my foothold in the ever-evolving landscape of entertainment beyond my hobby.

Carmelo Rodriguez

The conversion of my very first book into an audiobook marked another significant milestone in my writing journey. It was a moment of validation and triumph as the thoughts that once emerged, tottering from my mind to become words that danced across the pages, now found their voice, just like it had been in my head, to resonate with a new audience, bringing alive the narrative.

Days passed, and the audiobook gained momentum, capturing the attention of listeners far and wide. From commuters seeking solace during rush hour chaos to avid readers craving a new form of storytelling, the allure of the spoken word drew them in, one chapter at a time.

As the numbers rolled in, the audiobook struck a chord with audiences in ways I had never imagined. Record-breaking downloads and rave reviews flooded in, catapulting my work to new heights of success.

Beyond the accolades, there was a deeper significance to the audiobook's success. It was a testament to the power of storytelling, a reminder that my words could pass boundaries and connect people in more ways than I could imagine.

Seeing my first book transformed into an audiobook was more than just a career milestone; it was a moment where I felt deep gratitude and humility. To know that my words were being heard, cherished, and celebrated by strangers, people I did not know, all around the world, was a privilege beyond measure.

BEYOND LIMITS

As the audiobook continued to soar to unprecedented heights, I couldn't help but feel a sense of awe and wonder at the journey that had brought me here. From the humble beginnings of an idea to the dizzying heights of success, it was a reminder that dreams, no matter how big or small, had the power to shape our destinies and transform lives.

As just about everything in my literary adventure was slowly flourishing, I didn't let go of my past that had laid the foundation for who I was in the present. There was a time when the idea of the military wasn't more than an option for me to figure out what the right step was supposed to be in my life. But then I joined, served, was deployed, and saw combat, and everything changed. To say that I returned from the military to a different man would be an understatement.

The loyalty I forged extended far beyond the bonds formed with those I served alongside, sharing sweat and blood in the crucible of duty. It transcended mere camaraderie, embracing every individual who had selflessly dedicated themselves to the service of their country. The sense of duty was ever present; I was preparing to take part in one of the major parades in New York City—the Veterans Day Parade.

Yet, amidst the facade of perfection of everything else, I confronted an unexpected impasse in my pursuit of fulfilling adventures—a struggle to maintain balance. I was caught between the demands of my career, the pursuit of my passions, and suddenly, the precious moments with my family that were meant to be my priority slipped away.

But in the fraction of a second before oblivion took over and I lost consciousness, I had a rush of those moments snapping at me before I cascaded into the woods as fate offered me no remorse for what could have been even a fleeting instant of regret.

***

As I grasp a return to consciousness, back in the dirt and mud, a tangle of branches and foliage littering my new bed, the sharp scent of pine fills my nostrils. The realization of my inability to become vertical, which just struck me, now slowly began to bite at my spirit. Moments before, I'd felt almost nothing, for whatever had happened to me, it seemed as though I'd managed to cheat the pain, but realizing my disposal, a raging throb hit me in the head as I struggled to make sense of what had happened.

I must do that even as I grapple with my surroundings. My body's silent signals betray my physical limitations, but amidst the confusion of my fragmented memory, one thing remains steadfast: my military instincts that serve as my guiding light, cutting through the fog of uncertainty.

The mud and dirt beneath me hold no sway over my resolve; as a matter of fact, they're familiar allies. In the military, mastering the art of blending with the earth is a survival cheat drilled into my very core. Long armed with this foreknowledge, I press onward,

BEYOND LIMITS

crawling with a determination that surpasses the aching. Each movement is evidence of my resilience and propelled by my drive to survive, to last one more breath and the next one.

The realization of the pain gnaws at me with a greater intensity when, on seeing the light ahead of me, attempt to force myself up. It announces with increasing intensity that I am likely in pieces; even so, I manage to use push myself off the ground with an agonizing grind.

All I know is that I must find help. At the back of my mind, as the realization of the gravity of my condition intensifies and the pain I once thought did not exist manifests, the panic is right on its heels, but I don't let go so quickly. Being molded from the very mud and forged through fire from the military and life, clinging on to the memories of my loved ones with the wave of the countless things left undone, unsaid, and unshared hitting me, I tell myself that this cannot be it.

For all I've done and all that I've experienced, I feel like an unsatiated vacuum rising from the very clogs and dirt that were meant to cover me. Even as taking a step became next to impossible, and struck with yet another awareness with the entire weight of my body wrecked body resting on the plant of my ankle.

The reason for my inability to feel or move my arm becomes painfully clear as it hangs from my body like a rebellious appendage, twisted and awkward, appearing just a faint tug away from being fully detached.

Encompassing that moment, my consciousness picks from the background the disquiet that is unfamiliar with the woods and the source of the light, and I look from my arm at the figures that manifest and approach, geared and equipped as they race toward me. The sight of the paramedics douses my panic in the slightest, even as the pain threatens to quiet me, and breathing feels like the last thing I should want to do.

I look the paramedics in the eyes, driving right past their first inquisition to affirm. "I'm not . . . I'm not dying today."

Chapter Three

The stage lights and the camera flashes on the red carpet streaked blindingly, forcing me to shut my eyes. The reward for all my effort awaited me, much like I'd always dreamed, and all I had to do was bask in it. Be there, in the present, and enjoy the glamour that followed the success of a humble introduction into the world of Hollywood cinematography.

It felt nice; it was where I wanted to be. With my family and loved ones. Celebrating the stride and considering nothing as little. My gaze shifted from the flashing lights and swept amidst the sea of faces as I heard my wife's voice. Diana's cries seemed to echo from afar, distant yet hauntingly close. It was as if I was adrift on a boat in the middle of the sea, and her voice reached me from the distant shore, each call stirring restlessness within me.

I blinked, and the dazzling lights lost their luster, fading like the leaves of a tree stricken with an untimely autumnal sickness amidst the vibrancy of spring. My wife's voice grew louder, and searched for it the sudden haze, seeking it like a lighthouse in the middle of a tempest. The fanciness disappeared, and from a chaotic murmur, I peeled my eyes apart to emergency lights, almost blinding and worsening the throb in my head.

There's a ringing in my ear that I've been ignoring; it seems the least of my plight, even as I'm yet to realize the extent of what I'm in. I heard Diana's voice as I came to, face to face with the paramedics who discovered me.

"I'm not doing today," I voiced again, and they got the message.

With nods of accents and understanding, they hold on to me just as the adrenaline drains from my limbs and my ankle finally gives up on holding myself upright. "The—the helmet," I mutter, trying to raise my hand to reach it and instantly feeling a surge of pain that told me it's a terrible idea. "Can't breathe," I let out, even as the paramedics get instantly what I mean.

For the object that has most likely saved my life and was the reason they hadn't arrived to see my brain sticking out of my broken skull possibly, the helmet feels like a cage trapping the labored breaths. The pain that had been slithering around since my first moment of consciousness morphs into a different beast, this time taking hold of my chest. My breaths are shallow, and I struggle endlessly to get the air in and out of my lungs. I want to rip off the shield around my head; the paramedics help me take it off, and at once, it feels like I can dare to breathe again while I can suddenly feel my head. It's heavy, I'm dizzy, the throbbing has tripled, and my ankle can no longer keep up vertically.

BEYOND LIMITS

Despite my attempt to soldier on bravely, the paramedics' warning proves prophetic as the pain overwhelms me and gravity claims victory. Collapsing onto the gurney, they arrived, which felt almost like a crash, but the skilled responders swiftly maneuvered me onto its surface, their rescue efforts kicking into action without delay.

They talk to me, and I struggle to keep a hold of their questions. I'm clueless; I don't have the slightest idea how long I've been displaced or for how long I lost consciousness. I can remember my name and it sounds like a huge positive. Their words grow faint as I drift on the edge of reality. I blink once and there, and the lights return; the camera flashes diffuse into the torch in the hand of one paramedic. They communicate, but I'm barely able to follow. I hear phrases between "broken" and hospital immediately, and unconsciousness tightens it gripped around me.

In the presence of the first responders, the pain surges as the adrenaline ebbs away along with the blood I've lost. Glancing down at my arm, I'm met with a harrowing sight—it's practically in tatters, with bone visible beneath layers of torn flesh. But amidst the chaos, Diana's voice echoes in my mind, a lifeline I cling to desperately. I refuse to let go, not now, never.

A flaying attempt yields a determined grip on the arm of a first responder as I utter my mantra once more in case I wasn't heard the first time, "Not today. Not dying today."

This will not be my undoing.

Carmelo Rodriguez

***

The idea of "The Undoing" trilogy was conceived within the crucible of my tenure as a federal corrections officer. It simmered quietly, gathering momentum amid the chaos and whispers of the prison walls. Yet, despite its sprouting beginnings, the story remained dormant, as though waiting patiently for its moment to emerge from the depths of my subconscious.

Years passed, and I navigated a new chapter of life; the echoes of my experiences continued to rumble in my mind. While some memories were destined to remain locked away, permanently engraved in the recesses of my memory, others clawed their way to the surface, demanding to be told. Among them were the audacious tales of the characters who would come to inhabit the pages of "The Undoing."

My time within the prison system had stirred in me an acute awareness, an ability to discern the subtle nuances of human nature even amidst the cacophony of chaos. Whether I was physically present, little escaped my notice within the labyrinthine corridors of the facility. The trials and tribulations of the gangs that roamed the streets of New York and Baltimore—the notorious Salvadoran La Mara Salvatrucha and the infamous Crips—were etched into the very fabric of the cities' landscape. Even to someone not tasked with overseeing the most violent individuals on the planet, their presence loomed large. The shadow the gang life cast over those communities they claimed as their own surely did not end on the streets. There were times when it was clear that most of the activities of the gang originated from within the walls of the prison, where a significant fraction of their population ended up.

Rarely did anything unfold on the streets without the explicit approval of the dominant gang factions, and the audacity they displayed was truly chilling.

As a former correctional officer myself, crafting the narrative of an officer who was ensnared in the web of a notorious prisoner, a leader of the MS-13, tested both my creativity and my commitment to depict, as authentically as I could, the partially real-life scenarios. It was a delicate balance, preserving the elements of originality while capturing the epic and often terrifying realities of life behind bars.

It was amid this backdrop of simmering tension and untold stories that "The Undoing" trilogy took shape, meant to be proof of how the resilience of the human spirit in the face of adversity could prevail. But even more so, it's a testament to how a quest for redemption could take whatever turn as a matter of a single choice, either conscious or not.

As easy as it would be to claim that it was all the handiwork of fate, Ivan Rodriguez was fazed by the choices he made, choices that ultimately defined his life until the very end. Perhaps the only thing I had in common with the lead character of "The Undoing" trilogy was a shared experience as a correctional officer. I wasn't unfortunate enough to be tangled up in the mess of the gangs that dominated the prisons, and my adventures weren't as ruinous as his turned out, even if my choice of adventure steered me inches from the jaws of death.

It comes for me, and I know this a lot more than I ever felt in my years of living. If there is ever to be a description of someone taking it all back from death, my experience would be up there. I don't know for sure how the story will be told; beyond that, it will be, it must be told. My desire to live even as my body is in tatters goes far beyond me or the thrills and adventures I'm yet to explore, but for the ones that I care the most about, despite my choices. My wife's voice is ever present in my head though the ordeal, and imagining her face when she realizes that I have been undone by the virtue of being on my motorbike causes me to grasp even more for the breaths.

I hadn't come all that way to give it all up in the back of a transport. If I weren't going to be making it, I wouldn't have crawled with broken and battered limbs till help found me. I think to myself that I've come way too far to be defeated. But even as I keep reminding myself that it wasn't going to be my day, that I wasn't dying today, Diana's face plasters on my mind, and the urge to talk to her is suddenly untamed.

"I—I want to talk to my wife," I let the paramedics know.

Given all I have endured, the absence of my phone seems trivial compared to the realization that it is miraculously still functional despite the partial damage to the screen. As the paramedics retrieve it from my pocket and dial my wife's number, I can't help but feel a surge of relief.

My first instinct was to reassure her, to shield her from the impending panic. Yet, beneath my determination to persevere, profound fear lingers like a vulture encircling its dying prey—the thought of never hearing from Diana again sends shivers down my spine, pain more intense than any I have ever experienced.

With each ring of the phone, I pray quietly, clinging to hope amid the uncertainty that fate and the universe will, at the very least, not deny me the chance to let her know I am thinking about her. I am going to fight; I am far from the last station of my survival; death isn't getting me. I know all of this, I continue to remind myself, but it is just not enough to consider not talking to my wife. It feels like a missing piece in my gear for the battle up ahead. I yearn for her voice, for the reassurance that our story is far from over, that I will not draw my last breath in the back of an ambulance, leaving everything we planned, plotted, and promised tragically undone.

In a moment that sends my heart thumping and swiftly revives me, Diana's voice breaks through the ringing, and I've never been more grateful and sacred.

"He—hey, honey," my voice cracks from a partially heaving chest.

"Hey, babe. What's up?"

"So, um, I've huh. . . been in a bit of an accident on the I-95."

Carmelo Rodriguez

"Oh, my God. Oh, my God!"

"Don't panic, okay. Um, I'm . . . in the back of an ambulance with the paramedics and heading to the hospital."

The instant rattling is obvious in her voice, "Are you okay? Please tell me you're going to be okay."

"I'm going to be fine; we're heading to the hospital now," I reassured her.

"Which hospital?" she demanded. I can imagine everything else is abandoned, and she's vying to be there, possibly before I arrive.

"Jackson Memorial," the paramedic answered, and I relayed it to my wife.

"I'm on my way. I'm on my way right now," she said. "You're gonna be fine. You'll be fine," she reassured me, and I don't think of the veil of her shaky voice.

"I love you, Daine. I love you, okay?" I let out, not wanting to leave it to fate, as the tightness in my chest grew, and it became harder to voice the wind out of my lungs.

"I know. But you're gonna tell me that when I see you. And I'll see you soon. I love you," she answered.

"Okay." I nodded as though she could see me as the paramedic took the phone away from my face and ended the call. I cough and groan. Beeping sounds hit from some machine I'm attached to, and my chest gets tighter.

BEYOND LIMITS

The paramedics constantly tended to my injuries even as I was on the call, asking me how I was feeling as they glanced at the machine and examined my chest.

"My chest . . . feels a little tight," I managed to mutter.

It doesn't take long for the EMT to figure out what's going on. I had hustled my way off the ground, though I didn't feel any pain until my body wore off the adrenaline. I disregarded all the warning signs because I was determined not to be held back. The trudging was how I was going to survive. But the increasing tightness in my chest persisted. I had reserved my strength to speak with Diana, but now I grapple with the harsh reality that I'm losing the battle. Still a considerable distance from the emergency room, the EMT announced my chest wall was compromised. The words were like a sledgehammer I was already feeling against my trunk, and the looming threat of being unable to breathe soon became all too real.

"Your lung is punctured, likely from broken ribs, and it's causing air to leak into your chest. It's called a pneumothorax; it's the reason you can't breathe, and it's not good."

I could tell from the absolute hellish way I was feeling.

"We can't wait till you get to the hospital; we have to tend to it now, or it's going to get worse."

I nod.

"I'm going to have to puncture your chest to put in a chest tube and let the trapped air escape. Do you understand me?" the paramedic asked.

I nodded, "Do . . . do what you gotta do."

I'd seen my fair share of the several ways the human body could be taken apart and go wrong; there were injuries I'd only ever witnessed and never experienced, nor did I have any desire to, and having my chest cut into wasn't one of them. The paramedic kept talking to me every step of the way, even though I fought to hang on to consciousness. I was told before the scalpel was pressed against the side of my chest and cut into my skin, but it didn't make it any easier.

There's no denying fate. I know that. Life always finds its way to balance it all out. All the pain I might have escaped at the beginning seemed to come rushing back as, after the incision, the paramedic forewarned me that I was about to feel pressure and, by every account, it was like being stabbed in between my ribs. The pain shoots from that point to every part of my body and ends up in my head. For a moment, it felt as though the breath I was still short on was being taken away from me altogether. I grow wide-eyed at the roof of the ambulance, my face contorting from the immense agony before I finally shut my eyes.

As the paramedic's words that might have been of reassurance drift into the void, drowned out by the cacophony of my struggle, my vision wavers and dims. Clinging to the thread of

BEYOND LIMITS

consciousness, I fight against the encroaching darkness; I teeter toward the edge of oblivion, the very breath I hold on to a battle against the abyss.

***

Death's cold embrace closed in around me, its fingers like icy vines that wrapped around and gripped my very soul. It was as though the universe itself had conspired to drag me into the abyss, a penance for what I do not know. Perhaps my sin would be too daring to ignore the passion that drove me from the very beginning, to look life in the face and not be satisfied by merely existing and wanting more. Maybe my transgression is the audacity to live, to want more, and not merely settle for whatever came my way.

My reward was a heart-stopping moment, as I would later be told. Several following my vacation from consciousness en route and at the hospital. It was after everything faded into nothingness, leaving only the blinding glare of an otherworldly light that seemed to swallow me whole.

Unlike how many portrayed it, it wasn't just some metaphorical notion to me; the great white light was as visceral as it could possibly be. It was a bone-chilling reality that was supposed to give way to a glimpse into the terrifying unknown that awaited beyond the veil of life. Oblivion was beckoning with a silent, haunting call, with a depth I couldn't fathom and a grasp unlike anything I could have imagined.

Carmelo Rodriguez

I found myself locked in a silent battle against an adversary far more powerful than I could comprehend. For all my years in the military, the plethora of experiences I'd amassed in the art of war and combat, and all the skills I'd picked up consciously and unconsciously in my sojourn through life, I was no match for this, like a spec in the middle of a tempest.

I was helpless and vulnerable as I clung to life by the skin of my teeth, standing face to face with the pale rider who demanded I surrender everything. Or was I lying down? The memory is eluding me, you see, lost in the haze of unconsciousness. From inside the ambulance, when I blacked out, there are bits and pieces that I've grappled with, but it is with those that I know of confronting the stark terror of my mortality despite my vulnerability. All my courage, born of sheer desperation that had me haggling for a chance, fizzles away on the edge of an abyss.

In the quiet depths of solitude, amidst no bustling crowds and the comforting embrace of companionship, there exists a solitary path that each soul must go alone. It is a journey designed by the hands of fate, where the individual is confronted with the raw essence of their being, stripped bare of all worldly attachment. Here, in this sacred solitude, one becomes a mere whisper in the vast expanse of eternity, a solitary figure navigating the twists and turns of destiny's design.

No matter the bonds forged, the love shared with others, the riches accumulated, or the accolades earned in the realm of the

BEYOND LIMITS

living, on this journey, all things hold no sway. The traveler is destitute, stripped of everything that could mimic the façade of identity as if cast adrift in the vast expanse of the cosmos. In this state of unfathomable vulnerability, the only currency of value is the essence of the soul itself—a precious, intangible essence that transcends the boundaries of mortal existence. It is what it left, the final worth, that must be relinquished.

As the solitary traveler moves across the landscape of destiny, each step is loaded with questions and reflections on a lifetime of choices. Whether good or bad is a subject no mortal can answer. I had no answer for my choices because I would never be free of the stench of bias as I judge myself, as will no one, no soul, who exists on this earth.

This revelation transpires at the same time it takes for me to find my breath again. Amidst the countless frames that sizzled in my unconscious, it's an instant attachment to my mind, as a complimentary sticker slapped onto the soul that has seen what color death's garments are, a forever reminder that there is no Saviour beyond the last breath.

In the abyss, companionship is scarce. But if by some chance you catch wind of one, even if their voice is but a faint whisper slipping through the crevices of oblivion's vacuum, wouldn't you cling to it? Lost in the murky depths of unconsciousness, the first glimmer of familiarity is a voice, and I seize it with all my might, like grasping onto a delicate butterfly's wing during a tempest. It doesn't call me now, but I know it has. There's an instant connection with my soul that drives me to the memory of a time when that voice beckoned me repeatedly while I lingered on the edge of being gone.

Diana's voice sent an instant jolt that rippled me awake. I heard it; I seek it, and I don't dare let go until it is loud enough for me to make out. Like lifting my head from underneath the water, I hear her clearly, and her words are not directed at me; she's engrossed in a conversation with someone else, someone I don't quite know, a voice that carries no hint of familiarity.

Bits of the dialogue fall short of my comprehension as I part my eyelids to yet another light. This time, it's the fluorescent lights of the hospital ward. Gracefully, it isn't the white light, and I'm allowed to blink even if I pick up on the conversation between my wife and the other person in the room.

". . . We understand that in his medical directive, your husband is listed as an organ donor."

The words travel like a newborn monster that had merely been waiting for me to come to before harrowing me back into agony, but it doesn't just do that as it forces me to steer further toward awakening. When the pale rider had grabbed me by the arm, and there was no looking back, perhaps I'd be helpless to the conversation. I am present; I hear it, and as selfless as I might have been when there's no more for me to hold on to, hearing that what is left of me will be picked apart is not the greatest reception, even if it is to save others.

BEYOND LIMITS

"I'm not dead. I'm not dead yet."

It takes all to squeeze my wife's hand to let her know I'm still here.

Chapter Four

I stood in the Army recruitment office, my sense of duty and desire to serve burning fiercely within me. It was a pivotal moment, a choice that would not only show to others but also reaffirm to myself that I had untapped potential waiting to be unleashed. With determination coursing through my veins, I made the decision that would alter the course of my life forever.

Before enlisting, I ultimately had ideas in my head. One thing I knew for sure was that it was going to be far from a cakewalk because it was my life, and the lives of everyone else that was serving with me would fight alongside me. At Fort Knox, everything I possibly needed was instilled. With blood and sweat, grit and gall, the drills and the training prepared us for what was awaiting us when we crossed that line and stepped outside our comfort zone into the heat of combat.

With each training, we edged closer to the reality of the life awaiting us. Adrenaline coursed through our veins, driving us forward with a fervent desire to embody the ideal of a soldier and

BEYOND LIMITS

face the tinderbox of combat head-on. For some, it was about upholding family legacies; for others, it was about proving themselves; and for many, it was about the pride that came with donning the flag. It was two of the three for me—I needed to prove myself as much as I sought the price of wearing the American flag on my shoulder. Masked by the thrill of anticipation, I, like many others, eagerly embraced the challenges ahead. When the moment of deployment finally arrived, the adrenaline took on a whole different hue. As duty beckoned and I stood among the few who answered the call, the world beyond that door felt like an entirely different realm.

I touched down in Baghdad, Iraq, in August 2006, and it marked a moment frozen in time, one etched into my memory with indelible ink. From the instant my boots met the ground, we were thrust into a state of perpetual vigilance as we braced ourselves against the relentless onslaught of mortar and artillery rounds raining down daily. Fully clad in combat gear—vest, Kevlar helmet, and boots—I carried a machine gun, a constant companion that weighed heavily on my shoulders during those initial months at our deployment location.

As we set out on combat missions, each outing became a precarious dance with death, teeming with the ever-present threat of devastating shootouts and bombings that left a trail of destruction in their wake. The notion of casualties and falling mates had been forewarned since boot camp, but instead of the armless outcomes of the combat drills, casualties became a grim reality. This haunting specter loomed with each passing day. My deployment in Iraq was when being American-friendly was enough to mark one as an enemy, a death sentence that was meted out swiftly and mercilessly by Malaysian forces.

There were more accounts in which the brutality of that war manifested than I could repeat; far too savage for me to ever testify to seeing. I saw families being hunted down and wiped out for the mere suspicion of their allegiance to American forces. These were individuals who dared to dream of a better future for themselves and their children, only to be met with a cruel fate at the hands of enemy combatants. I bore witness to the harrowing scenes of assassinations carried out with chilling precision, with no iota of humanity leaving behind a trail of shattered lives and broken bloodlines.

One incident remains scorched into my conscience with searing clarity—a family of twelve, harmless, bound by their hands and feet, being executed in cold blood with a single, callous shot to the back of their heads. Their lifeless bodies were cast aside like discarded refuse in what was a grim warning to the villagers who dared to defy the will of those in power. It was a crude reminder of the unfathomable depths of how cruel humans could be, a gruesome display of the consequences of resistance in a land ravaged by conflict.

In the middle of the chaos and carnage, there came a time when I struggled with the weight of my humanity, grappling with the moral ambiguity of a war that was being fought in the name of freedom and justice. Many days brought with them a new test of resolve, a relentless assault on the spirit that had me questioning the very fabric of existence and the gravity of my choice. To deny how hard it was to find the beacon of hope and the will to trudge on with belief after witnessing the total annihilation of a bloodline would be an insult to both the lives lost and the audacity of my resilience.

To think that my team was tasked with managing the chaos of that scene—a mission that would be a test like no other—and that we were just as close to being the ones who ended up making history still sends chills down my spine and sometimes has me catching myself staring blankly into the abyss.

It started as a routine operation and quickly escalated into a harrowing ambush. Somehow, the enemy forces had the foreknowledge of our presence and stashed ahead of us with danger around every corner.

The mission was to secure the area and evacuate the deceased family from the scene. My team and I weren't completely oblivious to the possibility of danger lurking in the shadows, even if we didn't know for certain. We found ourselves under a barrage of attack. Bullets flew, raining down from multiple directions, forcing us to move swiftly and decisively to protect ourselves as we sought to give dignity to the perished.

Carmelo Rodriguez

In the pandemonium's head, a heart-wrenching sight unfolded right before me—a tiny body of a child tumbling from the bed of the moving pickup truck we were in. He was one victim of the senseless massacre. Without hesitation, one of my comrades sprang into action, literally jumping from the truck, scooping up the dead child, and even asking me for help.

I might not have had tons of experience under my belt, but I don't know how witnessing a scene like that could not affect a human being because, at that moment, I froze. I hadn't just noticed the bodies, but there was something about watching the lifeless body of an innocent child roll on the dirt that halted everything within me. It was as though a switch turned off as I stopped engaging the enemy and just watched.

In that pivotal moment, amidst the chaos and carnage of battle, time seemed to stand still as I bore witness to the horrifying reality in front of me. With gunfire echoing all around, I was helpless to my instincts as I was confronted by a scene that would sear itself into my memory for as long as I could draw breath.

As I turned my gaze toward the child in my comrade's arms, my heart sank to a depth it had never done before. Long strands of hair cascaded from the child's face, obscuring the devastating wound that marred their innocent features. A gaping hole, a cruel testament to the brutality of war from a large caliber bullet, was now where once there had been the gentle curve of a cheek and the soft contours of a child's smile.

BEYOND LIMITS

I was gripped by a profound sense of disbelief and horror that my soul questioned existence as time seemed to stretch endlessly. It was then as though the world itself had come to a grinding halt around me. The deafening silence that followed was punctuated only by the rhythmic thud of my heartbeat, echoing in my ears like a funeral dirge.

Alone, I might have succumbed to the attack on my instinct and reflex, and it wasn't until my sergeant's voice pierced through the silence that I regained momentum. His urgent commands cut through the fog of shock that was swallowing me. With a sharp jolt, I snapped back to reality, the sting of his punches against my leg serving as a harsh reminder of the urgency of our situation.

A heavy heart met a renewed sense of determination as I forced myself to push aside the horror that threatened to take over as I squared my shoulders, gritted my teeth, and prepared to face the enemy again. We ultimately escaped becoming casualties as well, but that mission had been successfully plastered in my memory, and there would be no "recovering" from it. There are few of my experiences in the military that will ever come close to upsetting me to the very core of my existence as this one. Perhaps it was the sheer innocence of the child whose life was cut short before it barely started or knowing that someone was supposed to be a fellow being had done that without as much as breaking a sweat. But I'm scared by the image of the tiny child with the hole the size of a fist in his face, and it haunts me with no escape.

Carmelo Rodriguez

***

An escape eluded me still—fast-forward years to my intense workouts. The driving force behind my dedication was twofold, and this had nothing to do with the military missions, at least not real ones. The grit of training was forever instilled in me. It's clear that I prepared for potential stunt opportunities in upcoming films and ensured peak physical condition for the tumultuous events unfolding in the city. Maintaining my fitness regimen was not just a choice but a necessity; it was a crucial aspect of my lifestyle that helped garner attention in the world of movies and film.

With each grueling session at the gym, I pushed myself to the limit, channeling my energy into sculpting my body and sharpening the skills I already had. There were two parts to the physical exertion: the part that needed to keep fit for opportunities and the part where it served as a release valve that allowed me to channel the anxieties of war and the pent-up frustration that simmered beneath the surface.

For me, fitness was more than just a means to an end—it was a lifeline, a source of strength and stability during chaos. I conquered not only the physical challenges but also the inner demons that I battled, those that had followed me all the way from the war. Often, the only thing that kept them at bay was the exhausting stretch of every muscle in my body. With each rep, each set, I forged a path to overcoming the travails I'd endured in life.

BEYOND LIMITS

In the heat of the gym, I found solace and sanctuary, a refuge from the storms that raged outside and inside. It was here, amidst the clang of weights and the rhythm of my heartbeat, that I found peace amidst the chaos—a reminder that no matter how daunting the challenges ahead, I possessed the strength and resilience to overcome them. Even if they chased me and occasionally, in between consciousness, I found that the quiet had only been a fluke, and the escape from the ordeal of war wasn't kind, regardless of how much time had passed.

I am reminded of this as consciousness ebbs and flows like waves crashing against the shore; fragments of memories from the battlefield surge to the forefront of my mind. Images of the war dance before my eyes, mingling with the hazy reality of the present as I struggle to hold on to something.

I bolt from these haunting flashes of the things I've witnessed, things I could never manage to speak of. They play in my head like a cacophony of demons awaiting my hellish embrace. Their grasp doesn't last as I slip, not completely. I seek consciousness, but it eludes me. The times I nearly came to my death have no relevance as there's nothing on the other side to latch on to. Regardless of my desire to live for my wife my family, I'm powerless at most when my will isn't enough to conquer the terror that my body has endured so deep into my subconscious. I have no choice, and so I'm at the mercy of the memories morphed into demons.

Carmelo Rodriguez

I see the faces of dead families and the innocent dead child tossed on the floor like a rag doll. I pulled back into that moment when I was momentarily useless and helpless to my emotions as I questioned humanity, only to be yanked out of it by the sound of mortar bombs going off. I'm haunted by the bullets flying from every direction and off fellow soldiers screaming from being taken apart under the rain of enemy projectiles.

It's jarring. It's hell. It causes my heart to thump and my eyes to part, but I'm too weak to continue, so I fall back into the trapping embrace of death's cousin. My breath is held mysteriously in my throat as though a hand had reached not around my neck but inside of it to withhold my effort. It's a struggle I'm unfamiliar with, even as the pain I'm in is indescribable. I'm the one to fight for my survival. Like footprints in the sand, the thoughts of my loved ones press into my mind before everything is yet again washed away by a current of fragmented terror, playing tango with blackout.

I don't give up, and for once, I scale through the hurdle and the haze of war memories to pick out the words in the distance.

On the precipice of a return, the first words that greeted my consciousness were the notion that it was impossible. Now, unlike the times before, my fight resumes.

"The chances that he's going to be able to come out of this are very slim, and given the fact that he's yet to regain consciousness, it's getting slimmer with each passing day. The hard truth is that we're not very confident that he's going to be able to make it out of this. While I know that this is no good time to bring this up, you might want to know that your husband could end up saving a lot of people's lives with his help . . ."

It's a vague summation, but I don't need the details to know what's coming. I don't wait for the meaning of the silence that follows, even with Diana in the room.

My fight had not ended. It cannot end.

I'm not dead yet, I continually thought as I reached out amid this tumult for a familiar touch that had stirred me from the depths of my oblivion. Groping through the fog of my mind, I quickly sought and felt the reassuring warmth of my wife's hand intertwined with mine.

I cannot let go; I daren't let go. I squeezed until she realized that I was there.

Diana's eyes were full of shock as she gasped so loud I instinctively reached for a breath as she sprang to her feet on my side. Even before I heard it again, her voice was a beacon of comfort in the chaos, and it reached me like a lifeline, a goddamn life wire to my soul, as she thundered at the doctor, "He's—he's awake. He's awake!" Her words carried a mixture of relief and urgency. The doctor's gaze snapped toward me, his expression a mixture of surprise and determination but laden with excitement. He was at once in tune with the urgency as, without hesitation, he called for additional medical assistance, summoning more hands to help access me.

As the room filled with the bustle of activity, I struggled to grasp the gravity of my situation fully. Diana's presence was invaluable to me. I struggled to keep my eyes on her, even with the medical personnel's bustle to welcome me back to life. I saw from the corner of my eye how much emotion it took her, how overwhelmed she was. Her grateful, misty eyes and her trembling hands were not so far from me, and as much as I wanted to reach out and hold her, I was temporarily helpless in the immediate aftermath of the greatest battle of my life.

The wars had long ended, but the souvenir of memories I had collected haunted me into my unconscious. The pale rider stood in the room's corner, and though I did not see it, I felt it. Its fingerprints were all over me like a tattoo, and I can still feel its cold, merciless breath rattling against my skin.

But I'm still here.

Chapter Five

To defy death is to stand at the precipice of existence, facing the relentless advance of the certain, and summon the strength, willpower, and resilience to push back against the encroaching darkness. It means realizing how frail human life is, confronting the stark reality that fate is a messenger of mortality, and still refusing to surrender to the grim fortune that seems all but sealed. To defy death goes beyond physical survival; it's foolish courage and hopeless determination. To defy death is to know that the end is inevitable no matter what, but to choose to fight against all odds to reclaim life from the jaws of despair and despair is to challenge the unchallenged.

It started with opening my eyes after however long I'd been on the floor in the woods as an offering to the massive oak at whose feet I had landed. My vision was blurry, and my head pounded as I tried to make sense of my surroundings. In all my keenness for adventures, exploring nature hadn't been at the absolute top of my priorities. I had always preferred the thrill of urban escapades.

Carmelo Rodriguez

Wandering through the wilderness was a rare venture for me, a whim of curiosity rather than a passion. I do not believe that I had any special connection to nature to warrant the oak receiving my fall in such a manner when there were a hundred different ways it could have gone.

The tree, from my hazy recollection of that jarring moment, wasn't merely a lump of bald logs rooted in a sparse area. It had numerous branches, many of which pointed heavenward and could easily have been the first point of contact in my failed battle against gravity. I could have easily been impaled as I was tossed like a rag doll into the woods. It could have happened in such a manner that all I would have had, if I had any moment at all, would be just enough time to realize that fate had no interest whatsoever in a challenge.

But fate did, and by virtue of luck and preparedness with the helmet I had on, I snatched myself a ticket for a battle against what should have been absolute. I began my defiance by parting my eyelids and breathing in the air, even when it seemed as though it was on a crusade to scar my lungs.

I had never once had the cause to imagine what it would feel like not to desire to possess a part of me. That feeling would come much later, with more than just one part of my body, more than just my lungs.

Crawling out of the mud was yet another step in my battle against the grim reaper. In the military, you're taught that sometimes,

BEYOND LIMITS

staying in a particular position could end up meaning death. This principle is drilled into soldiers from the moment they begin their training. It is not just about learning to attack or follow orders but understanding the dynamics of survival in the most extreme conditions.

On the battlefield, situations can change in an instant. What was once a secure location can quickly become a death trap. Enemy forces could be on a constant move, looking for vulnerabilities, and nature itself can be unpredictable. A sudden artillery strike, an ambush, or even the shifting landscape can turn a haven into a deadly ground zero.

Military training emphasizes the importance of mobility and adaptability. Soldiers are trained to read the terrain, assess threats, and make split-second decisions that could mean the difference between life and death. They learn to recognize the signs of an impending attack, the subtle shifts in the enemy's tactics, and the critical importance of not becoming a static target.

The thing is, in a firefight, the instinct to stay low and seek cover is natural. Anyone who has ever been in one knows this. However, you learn in the military, on the ground, that cover can quickly become concealment for the enemy. The longer you stay in one place, the more predictable your position becomes. Predictability can be exploited by the enemy, leading to devastating consequences. Therefore, soldiers are trained in the art of movement, constantly shifting positions to stay one step ahead of the threat. Staying in one place can lead to a false sense of security. As a solider, you cannot afford to believe you're your cover is impenetrable, that you're safe from harm. Such a mindset is dangerous and begets complacency.

Not " holding your position" extends beyond the physical act of moving. It includes the mental agility to adapt to new information and changing scenarios. As soldiers, we're taught to anticipate the enemy's moves as well, to think several steps ahead.

Historical battles give stark lessons on the dangers of remaining static. The trenches of World War I, for instance, became death zones where soldiers were trapped in the nightmare of a stalemate, left to relentless artillery barrages and the constant threat of gas attacks. In modern-day military, strategies have evolved to avoid such scenarios, focusing on the importance of maneuver warfare and the need to keep the enemy off balance.

To adapt is to survive. To move and keep moving is to live. A part of me might have known this from the common sense of life before or from an African proverb that says only an open hand invites a gift. I knew much of this before my unfortunate contest against Kismet. Sometimes, staying still could mean the end, much like how stagnancy in life is a harbinger of decay. It's as close to handing death an advantage as one could get, and I was not prepared for that yet.

Advancing toward the sounds and the light, even as I realized that I was closer to looking like an object taken apart by a beast, was

BEYOND LIMITS

yet another effort in my quest not to allow myself to be defeated. There was no part of my military training that involved standing on a broken ankle to keep erect, yet I did not just look death in the face but saw the helpers who had found me in the form of the paramedics because I needed them to know that I wasn't done.

I passed my message, and I landed on a gurney, but with all my efforts, it seemed three losses in a row was too much deficit for death to take, and I would find out that I was far from being an unworthy challenger, especially when it was fate keeping score.

As soon as I was secured, the first responders had to decide what to do after assessing me. Despite my helmet being off as I was not horizontal, it felt as though I was falling, as I was growing conscious of the pain of my injuries. I had tourniquets on my bleeding limbs, and the one swinging from my body was strapped back to it. Gauze-packed wounds I couldn't see, and casts held my broken ankles confined. I could faintly perceive the urgency in the movement of the first responders who shared their names.

Eva was a seasoned veteran who led my assessments. Her partner was Tim, who didn't skip a beat as they synchronized to help me.

"Stay with me," Eva called, making me open my eyes as I momentarily closed them as my body to signal the exhaustion from injuries. I did as I was told and heard as Tim relayed the situation to dispatch, with the conclusion being that I needed the most immediate lifesaving measures and judging by where we were—where I'd been disposed. The distance from a proper medical aid, an airlift was the best option for me to stand a chance.

I heard snippets of conversation as Tim made the call. Even when it seemed like I couldn't fully make out what was being said, I could read the expressions on both their faces. The airlift couldn't happen because the weather wasn't the most favorable for air travel, and the distance wasn't particularly favorable either. Tim broke the news, and it earned a guttural rebuke from Eva. Fate pulled one back, but it wasn't done yet.

In the absence of the fastest and best route to the hospital, the paramedics called for a full ambulance instead, which would have at least been better than what was on the ground—something more suitable for a patient in a critical condition. The response to that wasn't immediate from the dispatch, and in between, the thump of the headache resumed, and the pain turned up a few degrees with the adrenaline wearing off. I groaned as though on cue as the dispatch responded with yet another negative. This time, it was on the full ambulance, not being possible solely because of the location being too far out. It was one more for fate, and it appeared the pale rider announced his presence with the hand over my chest as the tightness increased.

"We have no choice; we're going to have to move him with the ambulance. " Tim's words, and I don't particularly recall them being exact, were the conclusion to the futile gallant endeavors to get me to the hospital as swiftly as possible.

BEYOND LIMITS

Eva's eyes dropped to me, and I remember the hint of regret that glinted in them before she announced it to me as she wrapped a final bandage around my broken arm. I couldn't really have cared less how it happened, so far as I was going to be on the move. Telling a man with death at his throat that his healing was coming through a wheeled cart didn't matter if it was coming.

It didn't matter how—whether it was crawling, limping on a broken foot, being carted in a wheelbarrow, or even carried by a giant stork—if I was moving, I had a chance. Stranded in the middle of nowhere, even with the paramedic and EMT by my side, immobility meant certain doom. If I couldn't move, I would become a sitting duck, and death would come to collect its prize with no more effort.

Eva and her partner bundled me into the back of their small ambulance, and it was fate remaining in the deficit. Between when they found me and when I ended up in the back of the transport vehicle, the only thing I could be certain of beyond the first responders was the fact that there were voices in the distance and lights as well. I had no idea who it was and what role they could have played, if they'd merely witnessed my ordeal along the I-95, or if perhaps one of them was there to take the count for fate.

As soon as the ambulance got on the road, I could feel oblivion nearing, even before Eva announced that she had punctured a hole in the chest to stop me from suffocating. It is quite how you might imagine it, nearing unconsciousness. Some say you never

Carmelo Rodriguez

know because you're, well, almost out of it, but even if the memory of reality in that instant is far from clear, the feeling of losing it is terrifyingly intact.

To say I was losing my grip on reality would be about the right phrase. With the pain now ravaging my battered body, I was driven toward and eventually past my threshold. I lay in the back of the vehicle, barely conscious of the details of what surrounded me, down to the color of the roof above me or the uniform of the paramedic stuck to my side. One molecule at a time, it was slipping away, and every time I grasped at it, either at the beckon of the paramedic or at the thought of my wife and my family, something was irreversibly lost, like putting together a broken vase with all the pieces intact, only it is not truly complete; it's not truly intact—there's always that shard, that spec of clay that's lost in the abundance of space, liberated and never to return to its previous role. And each time I fought to come back, not willing to surrender so easily to death's cousin, there was a portion of my reality that was lost for good.

When I opened my eyes, it was an image of being welcomed to my very own hell. The gaping hole in the face of a child, exposing the contents of their head, was right there in front of me. The horrific sight rooted me to the spot once again. I'd been squeezing hard on the trigger, exchanging gunfire with rebels and enemy forces. My body moved on autopilot, honed by countless battles. Even amid the chaos, I heard commands loud and clear, fully aware of the searing heat and the relentless assault as we fought

BEYOND LIMITS

to take control of the scene. This wasn't my first rodeo, but that didn't mean it wasn't jarring. The grotesque reality of war never lost its power to shock, no matter how many times you faced it.

The child dropped from the back of the van, and the body rolled face-up. The corpse of a child whose only crime at that age was being born lay before me, and my entire body was paralyzed.

The sight turned off a switch inside me, and when I finally got past it, the rest of hell awaited a massacre. A cacophony of gunfire and explosions echoed deafeningly around me, and I took cover. I felt the grip on my shirt as someone dragged me away from a position we had retreated from. Death had been after me for much longer than I might have recalled. The explosions grew louder, and the shots were never-ending, and the screams punctuated them. My fellow soldiers screamed; my sergeant screamed. Even as their vocalness was battle cries and commands, I heard screams that weren't so much as to order me toward life.

Voices of men, women, and children, scoring for safety or losing to the torture that used to be in the distance, were now right in my ears. I was right in the middle of it; they were right next to me. I could see their faces or what they used to be. Their homes and what they used to be. The air carried an unmistakable thickness with the acrid smell of gunpowder and burning buildings, a scent that clung to my nostrils and refused to let go.

Stronger than those were the scents that made my very soul recoil within me. The odor of burning human flesh is so potent it seems to rewire the brain of anyone who inhales it. Just as harrowing is the stench of death, a nauseating aroma signaling the earth reclaiming the life it once gave. This vile odor oozes from clusters of bodies that either haven't been found or haven't been buried yet.

I staggered back in a haze as I tried to get away from it all, and the escape that awaited me was a child standing lonesome in the middle of an empty village. Calling their attention yielded nothing, and I advanced, a cacophony of voices and a clash of commands in the background. I'm about to reach the kid when a loud shot rings out a split-second to take cover, and I look back up to see the child face-up hole in the head, and the terror resumes.

The images cut across my mind as the paramedic stabs me to save me. The pain from my chest is mixed with that in my head and the agony in the memories I hold. Fate cheats; death does not play fair. I lose my grip on reality and pass out.

It wasn't the end of it. I'm embattled with more of these images, even when I did not know where I was. The course I took from when I lost consciousness till I was parted from the first responders who saved my life would remain a mystery. Death cheats, but I wasn't giving up. With my chest collapsing in the ambulance, the deficit was reduced, and a level with death was no survival.

Then I opened my eyes, and my wife announced, "He's not done yet. " Everyone surrendered their attempt at giving up, and I had one more on my side. And so, the scale slid a little in my favor. But then again, it was far from the end.

The hard truth of life is that everything happens at a price. For you to become a conqueror, surely there must be a conquered. For every victor, a vanquished, for every battle won against fate with rejoicing, there is a price waiting, even if we do not see it yet. I fought to defy and came to just before it would be declared that my organs would be better off in other people. I opened my eyes and saw my wife again, felt her touch again, and saw the tears of joy stream down her cheeks. I opened my eyes as a victor; there was the price that came with it, and it would ensure that I didn't forget that fate cheated and death never played fair.

I woke up to the harsh glare of fluorescent lights blinking against the unfamiliar brightness. My surroundings slowly came into focus, and I saw one of my arms wrapped in gauze, pieced together by metal bars. My other arm was strapped down to the bed in restraints, preventing any movement. One of my legs was encased in a temporary cast, immobilized to aid the healing process, while the other leg was similarly strapped down, restricting any attempt to move. Panic surged through me as I tried to understand what exactly was going on.

Instinctively, I tried to speak, to call out for help, but I quickly realized I couldn't. A thick tube was threaded down my throat, making any attempt to talk impossible. They said the breathing tube was keeping me alive, but it didn't quite feel like it; it felt invasive and uncomfortable, and it worsened my helplessness. The room was filled with the steady beeping of medical monitors that, even though they were guiding my care, only amplified the alarm in my head.

I was given medication for the pain, but the agony that I was still feeling was beyond what my body could ever comprehend. I'd suffered a fairly shared knock and injuries in my previous adventures, but it was nothing like this. I didn't know it was possible to feel a stranger in one's body until I came to my reality. The deep, throbbing ache in my limbs and chest made it appear I'd been cast on the bed with a strap that ran through my very bones and pulled at my flesh.

The last thing I remembered was the chaos of the accident, the feeling of being thrown like a lump of flesh, and the searing pain that followed. I did not know how long I'd been out for, no grasp of anything going on beyond the fact that I was strapped to a bed, almost my entire body was wrapped in bandages, and the part that wasn't was bruised or swollen. I could move nothing: I had broken just about everything, and that was just from what I could see.

The price of survival was slowly revealing itself, and I didn't understand the bargain. In these first moments, I was in complete confusion, questioning everything. My surroundings were a blur, and I struggled to piece anything together. I was unable to speak because of the tubes down my throat as I groaned. Diana noticed my agitation and told the staff, and I was given a letter board to communicate. Lifting the arm even an inch from its fixed position sent a jolt of pain through my entire upper body, so much so that I wanted to retreat at once. Still, with trembling fingers, I painstakingly spelled out my first words, my handwriting hardly any fairer than a toddler's handle of a pen: "What happened? What's going on?"

The panic was growing within me, my heart was racing inside my chest, and breathing was more torture than a chore, as the helplessness was suffocating. Diana was there, her face I could never forget, and she signified safety and comfort, but I couldn't comprehend. Every second was an eternity as I awaited answers, desperate to understand, desperate to be free.

I'd fought death, and I'd come out on the other end, but there'd been no forewarning of the price of my victory, and to say it was jarring would be a gross understatement. Regardless of what I was being told—the response from the medical staff—the tube in my throat seemed like it was choking me; I couldn't be this helpless; I couldn't be dead with my eyes open; I couldn't be unable to fight. The more I thought about it, the faster my heartbeat and the quicker my breathing went; the panic attack manifested in a matter of moments. Despite the unbelievable pain, I raised my free arm, wanting to yank the tube out, and perhaps would have succeeded if I hadn't been stopped.

Carmelo Rodriguez

I wouldn't stop fighting; my body wouldn't stop struggling for comprehension, no matter what Diana told me as she tried to calm me down, and I would not hit pause until I was hit with a shot of sedative to hand me back to oblivion, albeit momentarily.

I'm served back to death's cousin from where it would watch on, and I would be reminded that defiance is no mere feat.

Chapter Six

Some memories never fade; they become a permanent part of you, every detail etched into the very fabric of your being. These moments come rushing back at the slightest connection, even when there's no clear relation, even when unprovoked. Moments like meeting the love of your life or witnessing the birth of your child. Times when fate is peculiarly kind to you. And then, there are moments like laying eyes on your very own Harley-Davidson 107 Fat Boy for the first time.

The meeting was a dream come true. I'd ridden for years and had my share of bikes. Without a doubt, some bikes give some memorable experiences on either end of the scale. There are some you would rather not want to take on after the first attempt, and there are pretty good bikes. You imagine life is better with such pieces of machinery, but this one, the Fat Boy, was something special beyond the fantastic experience.

The moment I saw it, there was a rush of excitement that hadn't taken over me in a while, even though I'd been on a hiatus. It wasn't merely because I was riding again, but staring at the bike, the flutter in my belly had me feeling like a kid who was staring at his dream toy, only this one wasn't plastic. It was the best assembly of fine metal I imagined existed. It was a beast of a machine; all power and elegance rolled into one, and I loved it.

The sun glinted off its chrome accents, and the iconic Harley-Davidson logo seemed to wink at me.

The Harley was a seductress in its beastly nature, and I knew this the moment I ran my fingers over the sleek, polished tank, taking in the matte black finish and the gleaming chrome. Every curve, twist, and ridge was crafted into perfection, so much I wondered if it had really been human minds that conceived the idea of it; if it had been hands like mine that built it. This wasn't just a bike; it was a work of art. The Milwaukee-Eight 107 engine looked ready to roar, and I couldn't wait to hear that signature Harley rumble. I knew this bike was built for the open road, and even before I sat on it, I'd pictured the miles of adventure we were going to rock together.

Climbing onto the Fat Boy, it fit seamlessly like it was made just for me. The incredibly comfortable seat was perfect for those long rides. The wide handlebars stretched out just right, it was ease and control at its finest. When my feet were set on the footrests, I was floating; it was one instance where I might say that I could glide and be ready for anything.

BEYOND LIMITS

When I turned the key and hit the start button, the engine roared to life with a growl that sent chills down my spine. That orgasmic sound with the vibrations was a thrilling reminder of the raw power beneath me. Shifting into gear and twisting the throttle, the surge of adrenaline that followed that would have knocked another man out, I tell you.

Just a glimpse of it, and the road ahead was calling, and with a twist of the throttle, I was off. The wind in my face, the world stretching out before me—this was more than just a ride. It was freedom, adventure, and a new chapter in my riding journey. In this chapter, I conquered my quests, every single one memorable, just like the machine I was doing it with. Life took on more color when I rode my bike wherever I went, and I never dreamed of a moment when I could want to take it back.

Not even the adventure cast me across the I-95, embattling me with fate.

Opening my eyes once again and resuming my reality, the pain woke me, and I emerged from a blur of the constant, slow beeping of the machines I was attached to. The sedation had indeed dulled me, but the agony hadn't faded, not even with all the medications I'd been given.

Diana was by my side, ever the comforting presence, and as much as I wanted to let her know how much it felt good that I was able to see her face again, the ache that I was in had completely taken over my body. No matter what I thought or wanted to think, the questions I had, or my desire, for the next few hours after coming to, the price of my challenging and defeating death was the seemingly unending reminder that fate wasn't pleased. I'd dare to say because fate cheated, the pain was still its tool. The consuming agony neared, and where I almost wished for a surrender for the pain to end.

And that would make sense, wouldn't it? To go against fate, hoping to win and defy death. One wouldn't expect a merciful surrender. When even the air we breathe tips the scales toward death, what is a baptism of agony but an offering to the pale rider, tempting him to tighten his grip once more?

Resilience is taught. It was a fundamental trait instilled in me during my time in the military. Every Tom, Dick, and Harry who walks the face of the earth has their threshold, their limit. My days in the military tested me physically and mentally, pushing me perilously close to my breaking point. Yet, I returned to civilian life, rarely reflecting on just how close I had come to my limit. The terror of those experiences was enough to make anyone recoil or even shut down completely.

Life comes at you regardless of the path you take. My limit in the military, shaped by the war, might have been past someone else's breaking point while perhaps barely scratching the surface for another. Resilience isn't just about surviving; it's about recognizing and respecting those limits understanding that everyone's threshold is different.

BEYOND LIMITS

Regardless of what I believed I could withstand when I was agile and able-bodied, nothing could have prepared me for the hellish price I would pay for cheating death and fighting to live. In those days, I fought fiercely and threw myself into adventures with reckless abandon, confident in my resilience. But the reality of surviving a near-fatal ordeal was far beyond anything I had ever imagined. The agony, both physical and emotional, was a brutal reminder that some battles leave scars that no amount of strength or courage can prevent.

If I said that I came close to reconsidering that battle, you cannot think less of me for it unless you were in my shoes. Then, to even think of wearing shoes, you would have to be able to feel your legs properly, move them, and not merely stare at your limbs as though they were simply accessories that made you look proper for display everyone to observe and judge, all the while what feels like fate was wearing off decades worth of adrenaline, endlessly flooding my body with pain, and the only thing I knew to do, only recourse I could take, was to use the one weapon I had left in protest – my voice.

I screamed. The pain was searing right into me, and screaming was the only way I could have some manner of balance. If I couldn't move and there was a physical enemy to battle, I fought the faceless one with all the might my voice could muster, even though the very tools of my protests were damaged as well. My vocal cords had been repaired in surgery, and the mere stretch was bringing pain, but it was one for the other, and regardless of how much everyone tried to comfort me, the groans, the moans, and the screams were the only things I could do.

I screamed to tell fate off and remind the disloyal harbinger that I was still there, that it hadn't won yet. My body didn't feel like mine; if I could have my way, I would have ripped the broken parts out if at all it would mean relief, but as I could barely turn in the bed, all I had were the screams that relayed my frustration at my agony and even more so my helplessness.

I lost count of how many times I'd been given pain medications to calm me down. Their only noticeable effect was a dulling of my senses, which was a temporary escape from the relentless agony. For hours after regaining consciousness, my mind was consumed by an overwhelming ache that engulfed every part of my being. It tethered me dangerously close to seeing life itself as an unbearable burden, a constant reminder that being alive meant enduring this seemingly endless torment. Every time, the pain got more unbearable, and I was hit with another dose of something to offer only fleeting relief, even that, on its own, threatened to break me.

In between, I was calm enough to appreciate a proper conversation with the people who had helped save my life. It had been a little over an hour since I was last given another dose of medication. Whether it was for the pain, I hadn't asked; all I knew was that my attachment to reality was a little firmer, even if the pain was still as fresh. The doctors walked in, and I managed to regard their faces; a middle-aged man by the name of Dr. Parish had been the lead on my case from the day I was presented at the hospital. Dr. Parish led the team of surgeons who pieced me back together.

I was asked how the pain was, and a part of me wanted to expel how redundant the question was, judging by how much I'd been screaming and how many times the nurses had had to come in and administer pain relief. But it was more than just a perfunctory statement. Even I was in too much agony to fully understand or appreciate it.

"Seeing you awake is delightful, really. And I have to say that you're one hell of a fighter, sir. Some go through half of what you did and might not end up as lucky," Dr. Parish slowly shook his head, "Your surgeries weren't easy; you sustained several injuries, both major and minor, aside from the ones to your extremities, and it's likely one of the reasons why you're in so much pain. I can assure you that the pain will reduce once your body has had some time to heal, but you must keep in mind that it's going to be relatively challenging."

I swallowed hard, feeling the pain that started further up in my throat as I readied myself for more. The pain had already made me realize that, indeed, I was at the beginning of the consequences of defying death; it would have been easier to mention what did not feel broken than what did. The agony had given me a glimpse, a foreshadowing of what I was facing. Even if my eyes did not work and I hadn't been able to tell that I was practically suspended, looking like a stickman with all the casts and the rods, the agony was enough to tell, but I still needed to know.

"H—"

I couldn't make out the words with both the throat that hadn't healed and the tube in it.

"Would you like to say something?" the other doctor asked.

I blinked, moving toward the letter board. Diana helped me with it as I scribbled my question: "How bad?"

I kept my eyes on Dr. Parish as he took a deep breath before answering. He had a look that suggested he was searching for the right place to begin. It was unsettling to see him speechless for the first five seconds. It was *that* bad.

"Well," Dr. Parish looked at me solemnly and said, "Just know that because so many of your organs have been damaged, you might be looking at issues that might be lifelong." He paused before he began the details. "You came in with a chest tube with a rib puncturing your lungs, the damage to your chest was a bit extensive, and there are serious concerns about your heart and lungs, though for now, you're still in stable condition. Your spleen sustained significant damage; if I believed in miracles, I'd say that was how we were able to salvage it. Your pancreas is also affected, which may again lead to some harsh complications down the line. You've got multiple fractured ribs and several broken fingers. You had fractures in your arm as well as your leg. Your back also has injuries in several locations—you had a very close call to losing the function of your legs, and your ankle is in terrible shape. So, you're going to be staying off your feet for a while. Also, the damage to your skin is extensive; it covers about seventy percent of your body, and your vocal cords are severely affected. With the extent of these injuries means that recovery will be a long and challenging journey."

And there it was; I'd wanted to hear it, and with every word the doctor ordered, it seemed as though there was more they hadn't said. Perhaps I should have stopped myself then, but hardly knowing was going to make any difference beyond deepening the frustration. I struggled for the letter board once more and added another word as I crossed out one: "How long?"

Dr. Parish took another deep breath before he answered, "Considering the extent of your injuries, it's going to be well over a year before you can see signs of a full recovery. We've had to hold off on a few surgeries to allow your body some time to heal, so it's not all too overwhelming. These surgeries aren't critical, but they are important for maintaining an optimal living status. The orthopedic surgeons will need to revisit your leg in the operating room to ensure it heals properly, and Neuro still needs to consult on the status of your spine. All in all, we're looking at the likelihood of two years before you can feel close to your old self."

Carmelo Rodriguez

I didn't know what I was expecting after I'd practically been told that I'd broken everything in my body, but hearing that I would not be able to live the life I'd fought for the way I wanted it for two years, maybe longer, and likely never again the way I wanted to be felt like having ice water thrown on me. For the first time since I could remember, the pain fizzled away in that moment as I chill ran down my spine in the new dose of reality.

The agony, of course, would return in the moment after that, and the medical personnel and my wife once again surrounded me. The doctor clearly said the expectation was that the pain would reduce soon enough, but then they weren't done opening me up—I was still looking at surgeries, which inevitably meant more pain. Despite the physician's reassurance that the pain was going to subside, it appeared my mind merely locked on the two years that had been projected for my recovery, and all I could think of was two whole years of feeling the way I was in that moment—helpless, battered, and in severe agony. And once more, it appeared fate had prolonged a real rejoicing over my defiance.

With every ordeal and adventure in my life, I built up a steadfast belief—not that I was invincible, but that I could overcome any situation if I wanted it enough. Each challenge and triumph reinforced this notion. The skills I garnered through my diverse experiences, both as a civilian and a military man, became invaluable assets. The relentless grind, the sheer grit, and the gore of the realities I faced and survived in the military forged my character and resilience.

BEYOND LIMITS

I learned to push through pain, strategize under pressure, and keep going when others might want to give up. These experiences turned my mind into a fortress, impervious to doubt and fear. This mental stronghold pressed in me the confidence that no matter how dire the circumstances, I could prevail. I was to believe that even if my body might eventually fail me, my mind wouldn't yield. I lived with this at the back of my mind for most of my life, and whether I was conscious of it, it was how I carved my path to survival.

It was still the same: me, fixated on the bed in the intensive care unit, albeit my body had ultimately been stopped, and my mind was now the one in the grinder. This wasn't the kind of pain I'd experienced before that could reach into the crevice of my mind for an assured answer. The answer, at that moment, was torment, and even if some time had been put into it, this was an adventure I wasn't at all prepared for, and I didn't know if I was equipped enough.

I was one to push limits in search of a thrill, never to the point of uncultured recklessness, but enough to know that I wasn't confined. My adventures were my living; anything beyond would make me no better than a lifeless figure. I accepted whatever challenge as it came with the mindset that my triumph wasn't impossible. And having looked death in the face and escaped the summons of the grim reaper, perhaps for a moment after I emerged from the woods, it seemed clear to me I was still unbeatable. My proclamation to the first responders was full of confidence and the culmination of the decades of my life that I'd spent coming out of the worst.

What waited for me on the other side, the price of my dare came with a limit that I, for one, couldn't immediately see who I was going to break.

What waited for me on the other side, the price of my dare came with a limit that I, for once, couldn't immediately see. It was a harsh reality check, a boundary that my stubborn spirit couldn't easily overcome. The extent of my injuries and the prolonged recovery ahead were not just physical trials but mental and emotional battles that had already tested the very core of who I was. For the first time, I was facing a situation where sheer willpower and determination might not be enough. This realization was a sobering moment as the panic lingered in the water, a recognition that despite my resilience and unwavering belief in my abilities, there were things at play that I was going to outfight quietly. I was one for pushing and breaking limits, and then there was one that threatened to break me, challenging the very essence of my identity and forcing me to confront the simple fact that my life was now complex.

Going from admiring and venturing with the beauty of a ride on the interstate highway with nothing but a handful of usual life hurdles on my path to drowning in agony, being voiceless, and not recognizing my body was not a change I'd envisaged. The surgeons' words droned on into the background for a moment

BEYOND LIMITS

after the two-year mark as I drifted once again toward unconsciousness. I could barely recall feeling the streak of a tear down the corner of my eye until Diana staunched it with her hand. Her eyes find mine, and in them, I was delivered a subtle reminder of why I'd proclaimed so naively, even when I am standing in pieces.

Carmelo Rodriguez

Chapter Seven

In the second volume of my trilogy novel, *The Undoing*, a character spends an extended period unconscious in the intensive care unit after surviving a severe trauma. During this time, they are completely oblivious to everything happening around them. The plans they had cunningly crafted, the lives they had touched, and the promises they had made are all suspended in a void of uncertainty. In this state of limbo, their role and status become insignificant, reduced to mere shadows of their former importance.

There is no striving for adventure, no pursuit of goals or missions. The thrill of the chase and the urgency of objectives don't exist, leaving only a profound stillness. The character's mind hangs like a piece of wet paper, limp and fragile, at the mercy of the cold, indifferent air. In this suspended reality, there is neither a hero nor a villain. Still, simply a being caught between the realms of existence and oblivion, waiting for the moment they might reclaim their place in the world—or fade into nothingness.

BEYOND LIMITS

Perhaps what is even greater than the unconscious battle for life is the character's oblivion to those around them. It is easy to vow to be there when times are hard until life presents a true definition of hardship. When we are awake, alive, and sane, we experience both the luxury of love and affection and the sting of heartbreak—those moments when the heart flutters happen because we are aware of them. The mere sound of a loved one's voice, the look in their eyes, and the feel of their touch ignite excitement within us, giving us a reason to keep going.

However, in unconsciousness, this awareness is stripped away. The character is deprived of the emotional lifelines that come from interactions with those they care about. The body and mind suffer in this void, each slowly falling apart or healing in its way, without the guiding light of human connection to aid in the process. This oblivion not only isolates the character but also highlights the deep impact of consciousness on the ability to endure and recover. Without the ability to feel love, fear, or hope, the struggle for life becomes a solitary, mechanical process devoid of the human essence that makes survival worthwhile.

Without consciousness, in complete oblivion of both body and mind, we're not there to witness the course our love has charted. We don't know whether our hope has found us or if we've merely lost. The promises made in moments when we were less vulnerable and at the mercy of our dearest are suspended in uncertainty, kept or broken beyond our awareness. When you're in a coma, you have no idea whether your love has remained steadfast by your side or drifted away. In this suspended state, fate holds the key not just to our return to life but to what—and who—awaits us when we do. This uncertainty adds another layer of struggle, as the battle is not just for survival but for the life and connections that might still be there when consciousness returns.

I could have wished all I could, knowing what I had and what would be waiting for me, but I am far from oblivious to how lucky I am not just to have cheated death but to open my eyes and find someone by my side. It's one thing to be an adventurer; caring about one, loving one, is something else on its own. When I met Diana, there was no hiding my affinity for the thrill. I might not have been some reckless adrenaline junkie, but I had my fair share of proclivities that would be considered tilting a little toward the thrill chasing. Diana was no recluse when we met; she still is not, but it is not hard to imagine how being in love with someone who is seldom in a perpetual state of adventurism could sometimes be demanding.

I see it in her eyes every time I get on a bike or must practice a stunt. I started a family and built a life with a woman who supports me in everything I do, whatever it may be, with all her heart, even if it must be after she's made her reservations known. Diana doesn't say it, not beyond "be careful," but there is a look in her eyes that sends me off, knowing that a part of her heart is perpetually strung up until she knows that I'm back home safe or within her sight. To love someone and build a life with them is to understand who they are and be at peace with it, even if the peace comes with a little palpitation now and then. The flip side of who

BEYOND LIMITS

they are, without their dreams, their hobbies, and adventures, perhaps, is a somewhat perfect image saved from the micro-anxiety, but a dull and domesticated replica that would live with a furtive smile on their face.

When one is confined within strict limits, one is exposed to a static, unchanging life. We already know what it can mean when there is no movement, no change in position—when, in essence, there is no sense of thrill derived from living. It feels like chugging down a bland meal to fill the belly, existing merely for the sake of living.

The thrill is certainly subjective, but perhaps the most important mission in life is to find what adds spice to it, whether it be a hobby, an adventure, or a grand mission. Just as finding that thrill is paramount, it is equally crucial for anyone who desires to experience the fullness life offers to find that one person who not only understands their dreams but shares them.

This person's heart should jump at the notion of you chasing your dragons, not because they would rather you didn't because you might get scorched, but because you are worth every breath they hold in their throat, breaths they won't let go of until you are safe, wherever you are—if they are not right there with you. There's an irreplaceable depth and richness that's added to life's journey by having someone who shares in your dreams and fears, who holds their breath until you are back safely. It transforms the quest for thrill and adventure from a solitary pursuit into a shared experience, making every victory sweeter and every challenge more bearable.

Alfred Tennyson was a poet in the 19th century, and though I know very little of him, there is a famous sentiment that is attributed to him and his works. It is the saying coined from the adage, "If you love something, let it go. If it comes back, it's yours; if it doesn't, it never was." Letting something go if you love it essentially means not stifling it because you fear it would cease to be or be yours when it drifts too far. I imagine caring for someone who is a bank of adventures and demands the same, but just like everything in life comes at a price, this is no exception.

It hadn't been lost to me what this truly meant. Before I met my wife and started my family, I rode bikes with a nearly carefree notion, embracing the thrill without a second thought. Taking nothing away from the family I was born into, there's a special seed planted in one's heart when they find a partner with whom they're going to share their future. This seed sprouts along a different course, creating new priorities and a deeper sense of responsibility.

In the back of my mind, I couldn't escape the thought of Diana when I got on the road. While I still enjoyed the thrill I sought, I now did so with a constant awareness and desire to return to her in one piece. The carefree rides of my past had transformed into adventures tempered by the love and commitment I felt for her. This awareness added a layer of purpose and caution to my actions, as the thought of our shared life made me value my safety in a way I hadn't before I met her.

My wife has always been supportive of my life and my dreams, and she's certainly one reason I've been able to come this far. The thrill might have been mine to chase, and the desire for the adventures might have been there, but there sure were times when life would interfere. Getting the Harley is one such example.

I had always felt that buying a Harley was a significant purchase, one that never seemed to fit into my budget—until, one day, it did. The dream of owning that iconic bike had always lingered in the back of my mind, but practicality and financial constraints kept it at bay. I window-shopped and, dared I say, daydreamed about that bike. I wouldn't say that I was obsessed with getting it, but I certainly imagined several scenarios with me having it and Diana knew it. Despite my desire for the machine, it wasn't a priority when it came to expenses, not a do or die, but as soon as I was able to afford it, my wife reminded me and insisted that I go ahead and get it. The realization brought with it the tiniest bit of hesitation when I wondered if perhaps there was something else we needed the money for, but Diana made it clear that it was indeed time.

My wife understood how much it meant to me, even when I suddenly tried to be humble with my desire, and she encouraged me to fulfill this long-held dream. With her blessing and encouragement, I finally took the plunge. I bought the Harley, a decision that elicited a rush of excitement and a sense of accomplishment that was apart from anything I had ever had.

She helped me get the Harley, and her excitement matched mine when it came home. There was no strict reservation on how much time I would spend with it if it didn't take away anything from our family. I would say that we achieved the dream together; hence, every time I rode the bike, my heart was always reaching out in gratitude to my wife for making sure it didn't remain a dream.

Indeed, it didn't remain a dream, even if a nightmare would attach itself to the machine and nearly turn the bike into a harbinger of ill fortune on one trip along I-95.

There couldn't have been a greater desire with my triumph than hearing Diana's voice, a tether I latched on to in my first full grasp of consciousness as I felt her touch and then saw her face. The gladness of seeing her again was punctuated by the panic that came with the conversation she was being engaged in, the realization of the lack thereof of my situation that fueled the panic further, and the absolutely decimating agony I was in from the injuries.

I was alive; I had survived, just as I had hoped and wanted so desperately to do. I had proclaimed my determination to the paramedics who came to my rescue, and even when I was out of it, I had been fighting to live, just as the surgeon had said. I had achieved all of that, ensuring that my wife wouldn't be left with the trembling in her voice and the horror of our conversation in the ambulance, wheeling me to the emergency department as our last.

Now, she was right next to me. The moment the pain eased, even slightly, and after being informed of what had become of my dare to live, my eyes locked onto Diana's face. She held my hand, her touch both comforting and grounding, as she staunched the tears leaking from my face.

Her eyes, touch, and words told me the same thing as she nodded her head. "It's going to be okay," she reassured me.

***

Even though I had been warned beforehand, it didn't make the news any less jarring when the time came for the next surgery a few days later. Being forewarned usually offered some advantage, allowing me to prepare mentally, but this time, there was a marked difference. I was no longer the same man I was before my collision with fate, and the change went beyond the physical state my body was in.

In the heat of the moment, a fierce resilience had burned within me, fueled by pure adrenaline that flooded my blood when I emerged from the dirt—a determination to survive, not to perish in the middle of nowhere. However, somewhere between battling the demons of possibly the worst memories I've ever had and regaining consciousness, my fearlessness had taken a significant hit. That raw drive to fight and the unyielding spirit I always possessed suddenly seemed to emerge under the weight of what I was now to face, as I had never experienced this before. This was a limit I had never crossed.

From my time in the military, I'd seen things that might naturally toughen my grit, and all the time that followed, hardly was there anything that could move me compared to what I'd experienced, yet the prospect of another surgery, despite the warning, brought a new wave of anxiety.

It wasn't just about the already excruciating physical pain that was likely going to be compounded after being cut open again or the daunting projected recovery process that was awaiting me; it was the sudden overwhelming realization of my vulnerability, despite beating death once, the knowledge of my mortality and the fact that fate hardly ever played fair dominated my thoughts. The mental and emotional injuries were as profound as the physical ones; my perspective had been warped, and every bit of courage I thought I had was being tested in ways I hadn't anticipated.

I was informed of the timing for the surgery, and when it was about time, I was wheeled away from the ICU to the pre-operative room. This meant that, once again, I had to part with my wife and family, even as, in this instance, I was conscious of it. As the orderlies moved my bed down the sterile corridors, the reality of the situation grew on me, and it wasn't just for me. Each time I was taken away in such a manner, there was a nagging fear that it might be the last time, and Diana had had to endure it.

BEYOND LIMITS

Yet again, I was about to be rendered helpless. The end goal of the surgeries was to restore me as close to my normal self as possible; they were crucial for my recovery. I understood I needed to endure being broken so that I could be fixed. This knowledge didn't prevent the dread from seeping into my mind.

The notion of being powerless once more, of placing my fate in the hands of others, was daunting. Despite the rational understanding that these procedures were necessary for me to heal, I was coming off the back of an emotional barrage that I had barely processed. On the bed, being wheeled toward the pre-op. Diana stood to my left, holding my hand to see me off, and on either side of me was the dread, which swelled with each moment of panic.

I knew that each surgery was going to be a step toward regaining my life, but the anticipation of pain and vulnerability made it hard to focus on the positive, even with my wife's face. Diana kept repeating that it was going to be okay; she kept telling me she was going to be there when I got out. I was supposed to believe her, but amid the chaos that my health had become, it was hard to see, no matter how much I wanted, that fate wouldn't dare to draw level again.

I had uttered the words "I am not dying today" with so much confidence, but lying on the table in the operating room now, conscious of being about to be cut open, I struggled to find that same conviction. The words were there at the back of my throat, but I couldn't repeat them. It wasn't just because my vocal cords were still recovering, and it hurt to breathe. Challenges were part of life, and this was merely another one. I knew that what lay ahead wasn't as severe as what I'd already survived. The doctors and everyone else had told me that. Yet, in this moment, facing the unknown of yet another surgery, fear gripped me, and panic threatened to immobilize me.

As I lay there grappling with the uncertainty of what was ahead, I couldn't help but question if this was my limit. Had I finally reached the threshold of my endurance? The weight of doubt pressed down on me, casting a shadow over the resilience I had once prided myself on. It was a moment of vulnerability, a stark reminder of the fragility of human strength in the face of overwhelming fear.

"Everything is going to be all right," the surgeon reminded me just before I was put under anesthesia. I wondered if he could see in my eyes how much of my fear was about to win. Moments before I would yet again lose my consciousness, a breath tethered me back to my wife's face, and I was reminded of all that she'd done, all that she'd been through. The thought of her being heartbroken stirred me to my very core, so much that I sought that voice of mine, silent as it may be, and reminded myself that today was still not the day.

Chapter Eight

I've always been fascinated by the idea that certain present experiences can instantly transport us back to pivotal moments in our past. It's not just a fleeting memory but a vivid reliving of the exact second when everything changed. These moments don't merely touch on our consciousness; they catapult us back in time and make us feel as though we're standing in that very instant once more.

Maybe one might argue that every second we live subtly alters our lives in ways too little for us to notice. Yet, undeniably, some moments wield a far greater impact. These significant events are beyond the ordinary processes of cells dying and the relentless march of our biological clocks. They become milestones in our mental landscape, their echoes resounding through the years.

Some memories are so powerful that they are the clock. They become part of our very essence, shaping our perceptions and reactions. They can intrude upon our consciousness unbidden, a constant reminder of a life-altering event. Continuing to exist is enough to trigger these memories, bringing them to the forefront with no apparent cause.

There are also times when the emotional wounds these memories represent inflict fresh torment, perpetuating a cycle of pain. In these instances, the past isn't just a shadow but an active presence, influencing our present and future in profound ways.

Such is the nature of our existence, where moments of joy, sorrow, triumph, and tragedy become the ticking hands of our internal clock, each second filled with the power to shape the course of our lives because torment and pain sometimes beget torment and pain.

The surgeon had been right—I had come through the latest surgery just fine. Surviving another bout of vulnerability was far from the end of the ordeal. Instead, it marked another milestone in a seemingly endless series of trials, each one a price I was paying for the ultimate dare—surviving.

I, like many, would have assumed that enduring another incision, having my body cut into once more, would be the hardest part. Little did I know, I had not even tested the true challenge. There's a reason for the saying that oblivion is sometimes bliss, and it wouldn't be long before I would quickly realize how critical that was. The military may have taught me that constant alertness was the next thing to having a guardian angel. Still, then, I would find on my own that there is a respite in the fog of unawareness because you do not know the hell that is the relentless mental and emotional and, most of all, physical torment some experiences put you through.

BEYOND LIMITS

Coming out of surgery isn't just about healing flesh; it's about confronting the psychological scars that each procedure left on my spirit. Every operation left behind more than sutures and scars—it left echoes of fear, moments of despair, and a reminder of my fragility. These memories linger, unprovoked, surfacing at unexpected times, serving as a constant reminder that my body is not at all unbreakable.

My heart was back where it needed to be, my leg had been fixed, and I had metal pins holding several of my bones in place to keep me from being a semi-solid human being. All of that was inside, and as excruciating as it had been to go through that, what came next unearthed thoughts in me I didn't know I could think of.

Having suffered road burns over seventy percent of my body, with injuries classified as second and third-degree burns, I was informed that my skin needed to be scraped and washed regularly to facilitate healing. Initially, this sounded straightforward. However, I soon discovered that I was about to embark on the most torturous experience of my existence.

Remember earlier when I told you about debriding? The process of scraping away dead tissue. It was excruciating, far removed from whatever forewarning I might have been given, from a mere discomfort. Washing the wounds prevented infection and promoted healing, but it felt like my nerves were being set on fire, so much so that in the very first session, I wondered if I was in hell because that was how it felt—like my body was on fire.

Feeling an ache in my body, my muscles and bones were something different. Having my skin peeled away from my flesh was an entire world of agony of its own. Each session pushed my endurance to its limits, turning the path to recovery into an agonizing ordeal.

They told me that it was intended to aid in the healing process, but what I experienced was nothing short of torture. The well-meaning words of reassurance from the medical staff did very little to alleviate the intense discomfort and pain that followed, and more often, it seemed like fighting a wildfire with a glass of water. Each moment was an agonizing test of my endurance, pushing me to my limits both physically and mentally, a limit that broke every time.

The one persistent song from the nurses and doctors was that this would make me better, that this procedure, this therapy, was a necessary step on the path to recovery. However, it was almost impossible to picture the reality, which was of the hopeful portrait they painted. Instead of relief, I grappled with a relentless onslaught of pain that seemed to defy the very notion of healing.

Even though I was conscious of how grit and grind in persistence and endurance make one tough to crack, being subject to a procedure that required flesh to be pried constantly felt like the opposite of trying to stay alive. I felt things I did not know I could feel. Every sensation, every movement, was a reminder of what my body had been through. All the benefits of the treatment, whenever it was being done, struggled to register and were overshadowed by the immediate and visceral experience of suffering. I might have wished to survive and subconsciously willed myself to it. Still, it felt as though my body was rebelling against the very processes meant to restore it, and what should have been a period of recovery swiftly turned into sessions of brutal labor.

It didn't take long for the line between treatment and torment to blur. I had moments that left me questioning the true cost of my healing. Yes, the cliché that the road to recovery is often paved with unexpected trials existed, one where the harsh reality of present pain tempers the promise of future well-being. Still, it had lost me frequently; I tell you this because there are pains one experiences where the very core of your belief is not just poked and prodded but completely crushed as though a freight train had run over it.

Memory had failed me several times before, but it showed no mercy during these encounters. I often wished for the relief of oblivion, hoping it might come naturally, sparing me from the need for chemical calm. Yet, as always, fate proved to be a ruthless adversary, striking when I was most vulnerable. It wielded my worst memories like weapons, attacking me with relentless cruelty that left me reeling.

Why else, as my dead and unviable skin was being scraped from my flesh, would I be reminded of the smell of burning bodies and the sight of corpses scattered throughout the village where we were deployed? If fate is not the cruelest keeper, why else would images of the burned flesh of soldiers and civilians from my deployment suddenly flood my mind at that moment? It felt as though I was being reminded that, although I had escaped that ordeal, I still needed to pay the penance.

It was what ensured that the torment was beyond the physical and was mental as well. Why having pain receptors on my skin constantly assaulted was not for a moment a remarkable experience, despite humans' ability to adapt and my somewhat innate skill to grind through the hell, an adversary one could not get a hold of, was a different thing entirely.

Amid the pain and the torment, I faced an even bigger adversary in the form of my thoughts. With all the ordeals that I had triumphed over, I had considered myself one with a resilient mentality that could get past anything so far; I was determined enough. I had broken my limit when I defied death after being slung across the expressway, despite the monumental injuries and the ache that came along with it, yet here was something more for me to defeat. While I wondered how much longer I had to endure, what tested my limits yet again wasn't just the physical pain but the absolute assault that came with watching my dead flesh being scraped from my body.

I arrived at a chilling crossroads where a terrifying thought consumed me: *Had I survived?* In between moments of the debriding procedure, I questioned whether I had truly opened my eyes, emerged from the depths of the forest along I-95, and been rescued. Was I alive, and had I been reunited with my family, or was this just a deceptive calm before a storm of realization, albeit without the calm? Perhaps I was trapped in a new reality—purgatory, a hellish existence with unending torment.

While I battled the pain in groans and moans with gritting teeth and labored breaths, I was voiceless to the possibility that this was all an illusion and my conquest over death never was. To the rational mind, I survived and was in pain that needed to be addressed before recovery. To the rational mind, the faces that surrounded me were filled with a mixture of gratitude for survival, sympathy for my pain, and concern for my recovery. To a mind that wasn't on the verge, everyone was real, everything was real, and I had gotten my life back, even if I had to hustle for it to be any useful to me. To me, despite my macho, I was quietly struck by the creeping thought of the possibility that none of it was real, and I had not even made it far enough to hear Diana's voice one last time.

That unimaginably morbid thought, which I never had in my life experience before, was a symptom of not just the agony of healing but the mental precipice from which I had arrived from having my skin shed.

There are pains one would not wish on one's worst enemies, and I genuinely believe that having your flesh disturbed and skin, albeit dead and rotten, forcefully scarped off is one of those.

If ever I could say that I lost my mind, it would be when I lay helpless on the hospital bed, moments even Diana and the rest of my family and friends were unaware of. I often wondered if the kind nurses and doctors who took charge of my debridement weren't real at all but were instead tormentors from my hell. They played their roles so convincingly that I was fooled into believing my life was continuing as usual. Instead of wielding whips and lashes, they held scalpels and gauze in their gloved hands. Instead of cunning and sinister laughter, they wore concern and attentiveness behind their masks, tending to every injured part of my body as part of a ruse plotted from the deepest pit of hell.

Such was the pain that I was going through.

It brought about moments when I doubted if I was truly amongst the living.

Day after day of debridement, it didn't seem like it got easier. Sometimes, I encountered setbacks when I bled from the dead skin being taken away, and the doctors worried. Of the several conversations the physicians and medical staff had with me when the debridement was at its most critical and beyond the pain, it seemed as if I might be ready to quit it out of frustration, as all I had to do was refuse the help, hearing something from the doctors seemed it couldn't have happened at a better time.

BEYOND LIMITS

I was reminded that healing was important. As I had asked, I had been answered about my recovery, and I knew already that the accident had left my body altered permanently in some ways, and I would never really be the same again. It was important to set myself straight with the reality of what to expect, which, in my case, was still plenty. Plenty of life, plenty to do. Bar the time it would take, I could achieve something close to having my life back.

That notion had me interested, but perhaps what made sure I didn't outrightly stop protesting was that it just didn't need to be done; it needed to be done right. Indirectly, I asked myself if I was still interested in life, and even if it sounded like a dumb question, there was something to it.

There was living, and then there was merely existing. Existing would mean surviving and not being able to defend my triumph, a waste of cheating against fate. Living, on the other hand, would mean doing absolutely everything possible to move forward while getting back as much of what I had before as I could, which was where the doctor's words mattered. If ever I hoped to return to anything close to how I was before the accident, healing was the only way to do it. It was important. What was perhaps more important, which many easily failed to understand and often made the difference between living and existing, was to heal right.

If my bones were not set and screws not fixed to keep them in the proper place, of course, they would still heal if the broken surfaces were together; what could not be the same was how the healing happened, and the wild factor would be whether I could ever use that arm or my legs for the most basic thin things in life.

Setting the bones and applying the screws would be painful and terrifying, but the same principle applied to every aspect of the healing process—it needed to happen for life to continue truly. Hard as it was to accept, getting my skin scraped operated on the same logic, even if I didn't want to see it.

It had to happen for my life to have any quality. If nothing was done, if the debridement did not progress and the dead cells were not removed to allow my skin to "breathe," my body could slowly poison itself. The scars would be unimaginable, assuming I even survived. This was the hard truth, a way of reminding me that the agony I was enduring was not in vain.

The necessity of these procedures was undeniable. Just as setting bones and applying screws restored structure and function, the excruciating process of debridement was essential to my recovery. It was a brutal yet vital step toward healing to ensure that my body could rebuild and regenerate with what I still had left. Despite the torment, it was to be the path to reclaiming my life, to move beyond survival and toward a future where I could truly live again.

Deep down, I knew this, but the unrelenting agony clouded my judgment, just as it would for any normal person. The torment was a cruel tactic, exploiting the basic limits of human physiology.

BEYOND LIMITS

Humans have finite thresholds, and when those boundaries are pushed to their extremes, they often shatter. This is the essence of torture—pushing a person to their breaking point. When that point is reached, something inevitably gives way. Whether this breaking point leads to a betrayal of long-held beliefs or the formation of a new, tougher threshold depends entirely on the individual and their capacity to endure.

Wondering if I was truly alive or if I had made the right choice in defying fate wasn't just the result of losing the fierce determination that had driven me all my life. It was a consequence of my thoughts being compromised by relentless pain. How could I reconcile my suffering with the comforting presence of Diana sitting beside me, holding my hand and smiling? In what purgatory would my family surround me with love, and friends continue to show up to support me? The contrast between the agony I endured and the unwavering support of my loved ones was perhaps how I defeated the question of the reality of my existence, which blurred the lines between hellish torment and genuine care.

Not being superstitious did not stop me from thinking that if this indeed was purgatory, then perhaps it was the kind of hell I wanted to live in. A place where, despite the agony, I could still feel the love of the people who surrounded me.

There was more agony ahead, and there would be no escaping it. Once again, I had been forewarned, but I knew better than anyone that this knowledge wouldn't make it hurt any less when the time came. I was in no place to look forward to it. Each time the dead skin was scraped from my body, a cluster of memories lingered on the sidelines, waiting to pile on the misery—memories I would rather not relive. Even though I had survived death and cheated fate, it was far from the end.

Fate found yet another way to play unfair, and I was unable to convey to anyone around me that I faced more than one kind of agony with each procedure. Every session was not just a physical battle but also a mental and emotional one as I tried to heal, clinging to the desire to live. The memories of war, the smell of burning flesh, and the haunting images of those I couldn't help save resurfaced with every treatment. As Diana held my hand, her comforting presence contrasted sharply with my inner turmoil; I couldn't bring myself to tell her that the pain wasn't just skin-deep. It reached into the darkest corners of my mind, pulling me back to the battlefield even as I lay in that sterile hospital room.

It had not been the first thing on my mind when I opened my eyes. Still, amid the chaos of waking up and grappling with the new reality of my life, a persistent voice in the back of my mind questioned the true cause of my torment—the source of the permanent change inflicted upon me. As I lay there, memories and pain intermingling, I saw the familiar expressions on the faces of my friends. They mirrored the look of the officer who had visited me once, probing to see how much I remembered that fateful day.

BEYOND LIMITS

Their concern was palpable, but beneath it was a shared, unspoken burden. Their eyes betrayed a silent sympathy, one that told me what I didn't know that I even feared: the individual who had done this to me, who had run me off the road and irrevocably altered my life, was still out there, nowhere to be found. This knowledge added a layer of emotional torment to my physical suffering, knowing that the one responsible for my ordeal was living free. At the same time, I was trapped in this cycle of pain and recovery. Since fate had already made itself to be the endlessly merciless loser, this, as well, was no less its twist. To be left to wrestle not just with my healing but with the unanswered questions and unresolved anger that gnawed at my spirit.

Chapter Nine

If anyone had told me that there would come a day when I'd have to learn to live again from scratch, I would have brushed off those words as mere cautionary tales. Life had already taught me the harsh reality of unpredictability during my time in the military. I witnessed comrades who once marched gallantly alongside me suddenly become critically wounded after a single mission. It was a stark reminder of how swiftly and drastically life could change.

As they say, "The real lesson comes when it's your turn to face the challenge." Or, to put it more politely, "Everyone's a gangster until a real gangster walks into the room."

Experiencing this level of physical trauma firsthand changed everything. It wasn't just about witnessing others' struggles anymore; my vulnerability stared at me right in the face and questioned my resilience. As a former soldier, I knew all the right words to say to someone who faced a tricky road to rediscovery, but learning it was my turn, the voice just was not as loud.

BEYOND LIMITS

After spending what felt like an eternity in the intensive care unit, it was finally time to be transferred to inpatient therapy. The major surgeries were done; recovery had officially begun. It was a milestone that felt like a small victory, even as the road ahead seemed daunting. My memories of the ICU weren't the most pleasant—not because of the medical staff, friends, or family, but because of the internal struggle and the realization of coming back to life.

During my stay in the ICU, amid the constant beeping of monitors and the sterile smell of antiseptic, gratitude was one of the last things on my mind. In those early days, it was hard to speak of it myself, even if Diana, my family, and friends voiced it for me. I was too engulfed in a whirlwind of pain, confusion, and uncertainty. Each day blurred into the next, and moments of clarity only highlighted how taxing the journey ahead would be.

The ICU was a place of survival, where every breath felt like a battle won, but also a reminder of the countless more to come.

As much as I wanted to feel grateful for being alive, it was hard to find joy while spending my birthday, barely mobile on a hospital bed, unable even to sit upright. The frustration of my physical limitations overshadowed any sense of celebration. Yet, that's the paradox of being human: the persistent, never-ending hunger for more. Simply existing fuels an insatiable will to strive for something beyond mere survival.

Carmelo Rodriguez

The road to recovery for me had been announced to be a very long one, and there would be no shortcuts to it. It had to start somewhere, and that would happen in the weeks that followed, which would be dedicated to relearning the fundamentals of life: how to keep erect and how to walk; how to use my hands, shower, and brush my teeth—all the necessities that I barely thought about when I did them before in automatic mode.

The first day of therapy struck a vivid memory. The sterile scent of the hospital that I hadn't gotten used to lingered in the air, mingling with the faint aroma of antiseptic. It wasn't my first time in a room like this; I'd been in many times before, visiting friends and fellow vets to show support, but being there as a patient was a different feeling, especially since I felt helpless.

Perhaps it was the eagerness or the fighting spirit in me, but even my mode of entry into the unit felt like a stake straight through my heart to my soul. I felt like a passenger in my body as I was wheeled into the therapy room, my body weak and unfamiliar, and it seemed, even before I made a single move, it was going to be an instant reminder of the trauma I had gone through. I knew everything I should about not giving up; it was a story that I had tried to instill in myself for as long as I'd drawn breath, but despite the mantra and the limits I'd broken to get where I was now, there was this milestone staring my right in the face, demanding that I prove myself after the milestone I had just conquered. It suddenly seemed better if I could disappear.

BEYOND LIMITS

I couldn't quite stay in that mindset, you see; I couldn't really do that, and that was not just because I was stuck in a wheelchair; I could barely operate on my own. Diana was right there with me, her presence an ever-present, comforting anchor. Yet, on the other side of the room, I faced a group of unfamiliar faces bearing warm smiles as I approached. These were the therapists who greeted and welcomed me.

Sun Tzu said, "It's well" in The Art of War when he stated, "Whoever is first in the field and awaits the coming of the enemy will be fresh for the fight; whoever is second in the field and has to hasten to battle will arrive exhausted." These therapists were ready for the battle ahead, and suddenly, I felt like I was on the back foot. I had expected to meet the therapy team, but I hadn't prepared for their beaming encouragement, their first "attack" that threw me off my game and made it hard to hold a grudge even before I got to know them.

Part of me thought that if I could direct my frustration at those who would inevitably cause me pain in therapy, it might make it easier to cope. I figured that channeling my anger at the therapists, who would push me to confront the pain and possibly relive the trauma, might provide a release.

Yet, as Sun Tzu also advised, "Attack him where he is unprepared; appear where you are not expected." Their instant optimism was a stark contrast to my apprehension, a tactic that ultimately disarmed my protest, at least for the first time.

Until then, the medical staff who had taken charge in the ICU had become so familiar that they felt like an extension of my family, a part of my being. Despite the inevitable clashes over the pain from procedures like my skin debridement, they were my lifeline. Leaving them behind and moving on to a new set of faces stirred a lingering anxiety in me. Even as these new therapists introduced themselves and explained that they would be my companions on the journey to recovery, I wasn't quick to let my guard down.

The uncertainty gnawed at me. These strangers, though well-meaning and encouraging, represented a new phase of my struggle. Their warm smiles and words of reassurance met a quiet wall with my internal skepticism. All I knew was that this was something I had to do to get back to myself. The road to recovery was still long, and I hadn't come this far to quit now. So, despite my apprehension, I steeled myself for the journey ahead, determined to regain my strength and reclaim my life.

The first step was keeping me upright. Having broken my legs and ankle and needing surgery to piece the bones and muscles back together, my body was not keen to cooperate. It felt like every second spent in a vertical position was a grueling contest with gravity, each moment threatening to pull me down. The effort required to stay standing was immense as if my body was rebelling against the very idea of defying the natural pull of the earth.

BEYOND LIMITS

As though that was enough, it came to taking literal steps with relearning how to walk, a task that turned out to be so monumental, I was baffled how I spent decades of my life doing it without as much as thinking about doing it. My legs felt foreign like they belonged to someone else. The first steps were wobbly, supported by parallel bars, the steadying hands of my therapist, and a gait belt around my waist, just in case I fell or slipped. Each small, painful step was a victory, a testament to resilience, but also a painful reminder of how far I had to go.

While staying erect and moving around was a nearly impossible task, there was using my hands again, which was another challenge. Ever since the accident, my limbs had become mere appendages, attachments to my body that merely functioned. Things as simple as gripping a spoon to feed myself or buttoning my shirt had become hardly feasible. To raise my arm chest level brought so much distress; it was an achievement if I could manage it. The pain from my hands radiated throughout my body, and my muscles ached.

My fingers, once nimble and precise, capable of mastering any craft from riding a bike to wielding a rifle, now trembled like a leaf in the wind, filled with uncertainty. The trembling of my hands was a stark contrast to the skillfulness and precision that had once defined me. Compared to the stunts and feats I had effortlessly performed, this was no willing trick but a cruel reminder of my current fragility.

Carmelo Rodriguez

What lay ahead of me were countless hours of practicing the same things I used to do effortlessly. Even before I made efforts, the frustration hovered like a night stalker, mounting with each failed attempt. The therapists seemed to have sensed my anxiety; they were prepared to be patient, to guide me through each step, and to remind me that progress, no matter how slow, was still progressing.

My vulnerability went beyond the skills I could no longer perform with my hands or the fanciful steps I could no longer make; the most basic of things that mattered as much as my dignity, I could no longer control. Showering and brushing my teeth were insurmountable obstacles I could no longer conquer on my own, and I needed the help of Diana. I could no longer stand in the shower; the warm water cascading over me met me without balance as my legs shook under the weight of my body, and I would instantly collapse if I had no support. Brushing my teeth, an act so mundane and routine, turned into an exercise in patience and perseverance.

From the first day in therapy, which was beyond grueling, another test, to the limits of my physical and mental endurance, I was being instilled with the mindset that, between the pain and frustration, there would be moments of triumph. I was made to picture the first time I would stand up unaided again, the first time I would button my shirt without assistance when I could walk across the room on my own again to pick up my kid. Picturing each milestone had stirred me truly. They were all things I was desperate to do again, things I had thought of countless times during my stay in the ICU, but being reminded that it was possible by the therapists provided a slight ray of hope, a reminder that I was on the path to reclaiming my life.

For this journey, I had the unwavering support of my family and friends awaiting me. They were there for every small victory and setback, their presence a source of strength and motivation. Diana was my rock. She held my hand through the toughest moments; her smile was a constant reminder of why I was fighting so hard to heal.

The beginning weeks in inpatient therapy were some of the most challenging times of my life, and I had little idea how much it would change me.

***

I have mentioned perhaps more than once how, with every milestone since cheating death, one pain outgrew the other. How a feeling was different from everything and anything else I had ever had. There is one wrench to the heart that was the greatest of all: the straw that nearly took out my road-torn camel.

When it came down to it, I was okay with enduring everything I faced. It was just another challenge for me to overcome, and no matter how hard it might have been, I knew it was for my good. I could handle whatever came my way. What I couldn't handle was watching my family suffer as I navigated this drastic change in my life. That, perhaps, was the part of this incident that broke my heart the most. Beyond not being able to live as I used to and struggling to recognize myself, the most terrifying and disheartening aspect was seeing my family and my kids so confused they couldn't recognize me. I was different, and they knew it. They saw it! Helplessness encamped me at seeing their faces with me like this.

As much as I enjoyed adventures and the thrill of exploring, I lived for my family. My wife and kids were my everything, and there was nothing I wouldn't do for them. I prided myself on being a father who was not just a protector and provider but also someone my children felt safe and open. It was my life's goal that they would never hesitate to come to me with anything. One thing I hadn't anticipated was how deeply my condition would impact them.

The pinnacle of my frustration and heartbreak was realizing my toddler was terrified of me. Seeing the panic in his eyes when he looked at me was devastating. Before the accident, he couldn't get enough of me. But now, Mat was too scared to touch or even look at me. He would say, "That's not my daddy," and no matter how much anyone tried to convince him otherwise, his denial was absolute. It was painful, and no one could blame him, especially me.

How could I blame my toddler for not recognizing me when I, myself, was struggling to recognize the person I had become? With eighty percent of my body wrapped in bandages, I looked more like a mummy than a man. I had come so close to death, and accepting my fragility was a battle I was still fighting. Seeing Mat's fear and hearing his words cut deeper than any physical pain I had endured.

I had always believed I was strong enough to overcome anything, but this—this was different. This was a wound that didn't heal with time or treatment. Watching my family, especially Mat, struggle to come to terms with what had happened to me was a pain I had never anticipated. I saw it on my older two as well. My older children, though trying to be brave, were not untouched by the ordeal. They put on a brave face, but I could see the fear in their eyes and the hesitation in their steps when they approached my bed. I wanted to reassure them, to tell them that everything would be okay, but how could I when I wasn't sure of it myself? The man they looked up to, their hero, was now reduced to a shadow of his former self—the guilt of causing them such distress gnawed at me relentlessly.

The once lively confluence of my family was now shrouded in heavy silence, broken only by the beeping of medical machines and the hushed interruptions of medical staff.

Their confusion, their fear, and their heartbreak became my own. Each day brought a new wave of challenges, not just physical but emotional. Diana tried to stay strong, but I could see the toil it was taking on her. The strain of caring for me, of explaining to our son why their father looked so different, was wearing her down.

Carmelo Rodriguez

In the quiet moments of the night, when the painkillers dulled my physical agony but couldn't touch the emotional torment, I heard soft sobs next to me. Diana thought I was asleep and that I couldn't hear her torment, but I did. It crushed me. To think that I was supposed to be her rock, the one who protected her from the world, and now I was the source of her deepest sorrow.

When therapy began, each day was a struggle, not just against my physical limitations but against the overwhelming sadness that threatened to consume me. The therapists, kind and encouraging, were a lifeline, but even they couldn't touch the deeper wounds. Remembering my toddler's words and my kids' reaction forced me to push myself, not just for my sake, but for my family's. They needed to see that I could get better, that there was hope.

Hope was a fragile thing. Setbacks accompanied every small victory. The first time I stood on my own, even if for just a few seconds, was a triumph, but the pain that followed was a brutal reminder of how far I still had to go. Through it all, the image of my children's frightened faces haunted me, driving me to push harder, even when every fiber of my being screamed for relief.

As it was, I understood it wasn't just my body that needed healing but my spirit. The journey ahead was so long and uncertain, filled with obstacles I had yet to imagine. My cheating death and getting one over fate had not ended; it had come at a price that was far from pleasant, and even if I could be alright with dealing with my physical dents, something more propelled me. For the sake of my

BEYOND LIMITS

family, for the love I had for them, I knew I had to keep going. No matter how hard the road, no matter how deep the pain, I had to break whatever limit to be the father and husband that my family needed, the man I once was.

Chapter Ten

I had seen the desert stretch out before me, an endless sea of sand that seemed to swallow everything in its path, including time itself. Life, regardless of its coordinates or circumstances, is a form of art. Whether you're in a desert or a bustling city, on a mission or at rest, the essence of life remains an intricate masterpiece. While the moments of my deployment that I could cherish were few and far between, it wasn't for lack of desire to find something beyond the horror of a war-torn land.

There's a phrase that goes something like, "You blink, and you miss out on the rest of your life." I closed my eyes, and everything turned on its head. Days and nights blended into a perpetual blur of golden heat and inky darkness. Whether I had a watch to guide me was, for lack of a better word, pointless. Time seemed frozen, locked in a silent protest against the relentless sun.

Hour after hour, we'd been out on patrol for what felt like an eternity, though in reality, it had only been a few days. The mission consumed me, the objective, an ever-present whisper in my mind

BEYOND LIMITS

as my team and I moved like ghosts through the thick jungle. My senses, honed to a razor's edge, suffered as my awareness of the passage of time dulled to nothing.

In the heat of the battle against insurgents, my unit and I went through a phase where we were running missions so often we could not decipher what day it was or even the time. The relentless pace turned days into nights and nights into days. We would return to our area to sleep, shower, eat, and prepare for the next mission in an endless cycle of survival.

One morning, we received a notification that changed everything. A team from the overnight shift had been slaughtered; some were kidnapped. They had been ambushed, and some soldiers were killed on-site, their bodies rigged as booby traps, while others were taken captive. Our mission abruptly shifted focus to rescuing the remaining members of that team, dead or alive.

"Dead or alive." I never liked that phrase. The idea that death was an acceptable outcome for brave soldiers who marched into battle never sat right with me. Soldiers are indeed prepared to give their lives for their country, and many American military men and women have done so. Yet, to think of death as an acceptable sacrifice simply because it is the ultimate one seems rather fickle.

Unless fate dictates otherwise, the fight should always be pursued with a mindset of victory and the hope to live to see it. Only then can it be said that the true limit has been reached. The alternative diminishes the value of survival and the spirit of those who fight.

For me, the true measure of a soldier's bravery is not just in the willingness to face death but in the unyielding desire to live, to overcome, and to continue the fight. Then, and only then, could a limit be truly broken.

Determined to find the missing allies and other squad members, we descended into 18 to 24-hour operations. While the picture of us flying through villages and cities in Blackhawks, following every lead, and raiding as many locations as possible sounds like the fragments of the idea for a top action movie, the reality was anything but as scripted, and hardly was it ever. The reality was desperation, concern, and worry laced behind every atom of grit that we showed.

The urgency and intensity of our mission were palpable. Each operation blended into the next, a persistent pursuit driven by the hope of bringing our comrade home.

It was one period when time genuinely no longer had meaning. Everything was defined by the mission, the objective, and the unyielding determination to find and bring our brothers back. The unknown stretched out before us, a constant reminder of the vast, indifferent landscape we navigated. Amid the chaos, there was a strange, haunting beauty in the endless nature, like the sea of sand, a stark contrast to the turmoil within, even if it all would soon be tainted in the most grueling way possible.

Regardless of our intentions as humans, life and nature are innocent, even in the depths of the wild. It is our ventures, actions, greed, desires, and thoughtlessness that bring about all kinds of realizations. Perhaps it's the adventurer in me that, for a moment, felt sentimental about life in a different part of the world, but that was before witnessing the devastation of war. Like every other soldier forged from the heat and fire of U.S. Army training, I was far from oblivious to what to expect when deployed. I might not have known exactly what our enemies would do every single time, but we knew what they were capable of, and war was never, ever pleasant.

Carrying that mindset, along with that of an adventurer, allowed me to see the world most dynamically. Perhaps it was why, in the end, it was more disheartening. There's a difference between being a clueless pacifist, unaware that bad people exist and do terrible things, and being someone who genuinely desires to appreciate life and nature through the eyes of someone who has seen a different world.

Being a soldier doesn't strip away one's appreciation for the beauty and complexity of life. On the contrary, it can amplify it. When you've seen the worst humanity can offer, the simple, innocent aspects of life become even more precious. The contrast between the serene and the horrific sharpens your awareness, making you long for peace even as you prepare for conflict. This duality of being both a protector and an observer is what makes the dissonance of war and nature so striking.

Carmelo Rodriguez

Every mission, every encounter, carries this dual perspective. You move through foreign landscapes with a tactical mind, but there's a part of you that can't help but notice the beauty in a sunset or the resilience in the eyes of a child. It's this complexity that makes the experience both enriching and deeply sorrowful. The adventurer in me wanted to embrace the world, while the soldier in me had to confront its darkest realities. This is the dichotomy that shapes every soldier who dares to dream beyond the battlefield.

When I joined the military, I did so because I needed to prove to everyone, and myself, that I had more chapters in my life to explore; that I could still do more. I signed up for the army with the notion of serving my country but also with the desire to experience an adventure that could never come from the streets and regular daily life my heart often yearned for. Had I desired too much? Bitten off more than I could chew? Asked for the mess I saw of the world afterward? Those answers truly elude me.

Would I have had a better life if I had turned around, walked out of that recruitment office, and abandoned any notion of becoming memorable for my country? How could I ever tell? How could anyone? There are, quite literally, infinite decisions one could make with one breath and, in the blink of an eye, any of which could alter the course of one's life. Who is to tell how the altering happens and which way it goes from then on? A hundred different things could have taken the place of my decision to join the army, and imagining all that would have meant in a different time would have meant I did not get to see the world for what it was: the beauty and the chaos, every ordeal that pulled so tightly at my thoughts and heartstrings to forge me into what I would end up becoming; to create that spirit of resilience, to survive what was coming, quite literally, down the road.

Joining the military was a leap into the unknown, a chance to push beyond the mundane and discover a sense of purpose and adventure that daily life couldn't offer. Every decision leading up to that moment felt like a step toward something greater, something that would define me. The challenges and the camaraderie, the harsh realities of war, and the moments of unexpected beauty all shaped me in ways I could never have expected. I witnessed the world's extremes, both its splendor and its savagery, and these experiences carved out a resilience in me, a deep-seated strength that I now carry with me.

Could I have foreseen the toll it would take on me and my loved ones? The pain, the loss, and the enduring scars, both seen and unseen. Probably not. Looking back, I see that every step every decision, brought me to where I am now, equipped to face whatever comes next with a fortitude I might not have had otherwise. This journey, with all its highs and lows, has been my path to understanding myself and my place in the world, even as I continue to question and learn from it.

Maybe there is a universe in which a version of me makes the opposite of every life-changing decision I ever made, and as interesting as it is to imagine what the result is, I can't help but feel like I already know. The clear truth is that every decision, big or small, is tied to my very being. The same boy whose eyes lit up the first time he saw a bike and desired to see the open road with it was the same one who chose to be part of the military. That same man chose Diana as the love of his life, was the same man who got on his Harley on the I-95. Anything but those decisions and countless others not revealed here would not be genuinely me.

I could imagine that my alter ego chose a reserved and sedentary life and was maybe happy with his uneventful days, but I don't believe for a second that he would be me. He wouldn't have my wife and partner as I do in my life because, ultimately, that version of me was who she fell in love with.

Each decision I made was an extension of my true self, an expression of my desires, fears, and dreams. The adventures I sought, the battles I fought, and the love I found in Diana were all threads woven into the fabric of who I am. Without these threads, the tapestry of my life would be incomplete, the depth and richness that define my existence.

There is comfort in knowing that, despite the trials and tribulations, I have lived authentically. The scars I bear, both physical and emotional, are testaments to a life fully lived, not merely endured. They are reminders of the roads I traveled, the choices I made, and the resilience I found within myself.

BEYOND LIMITS

In this universe, I am the sum of my experiences, and I wouldn't trade them for the uncertainty of another path. The what-ifs and maybes can linger in my mind, but they can never replace the reality of the life I've built and the love I've found. This journey, with all its highs and lows, is mine and mine alone, and I embrace it with every fiber of my being.

There's a paradox in the unknown: it offers safety even as it terrifies. It's unknown because it's uncharted, and some people choose it precisely for that reason. While a life where nothing happens might shield one from the pain and ordeals that have shaped my existence, it would also mean a life devoid of adventures, dreams, and desires. It would be a life where I would never discover my limits because I would never do enough to find out. The notion of living passively, "taking it as it comes," without striving to survive, feels like an assault on my very essence. I say this after everything I've endured; this realization comes as I simmer in the consequences of defying fate and refusing to let death claim me.

There's a profound difference between merely fearing death and facing it. To be near death is to have, at some point, truly lived—not just existed. Real death, not just the cessation of breath, is something only those who have marked their lives with meaningful moments and memories can understand. My struggle against dying revealed to me I had lived a life worth fighting for, a life I was unwilling to relinquish, no matter how hard the fight or how tempting the ease of letting go was.

Cheating death doesn't always guarantee life. This is one of the priceless lessons I would learn down the road, even in my early days of reveling in my victory against fate. Life has a way of confronting you with your own words, actions, and thoughts. Your memories, which once defined you, now stand in your way when you take a second charge at life.

Every step forward is shadowed by the past, by the man I used to be and the man I am striving to become. The battle isn't just physical; it's mental and emotional. The echoes of my past victories and failures taunt me, questioning my strength and resolve. It's one thing to have survived the immediate peril. Still, it's another to face the relentless challenge of redefining oneself, of piecing together a life from the fragments left after the storm.

Every milestone achieved is a reminder of what was lost and what is yet to be regained. The struggle is ongoing, a continuous journey of overcoming not just the scars on my body but the deeper, invisible ones etched into my soul. As I navigate this second chance in life, I'm learning that the greatest battle is within, where the ghosts of my past meet the uncertainty of my future.

For me, survival wasn't just about breathing; it was about reclaiming the life I had fought so hard to preserve. Every milestone, every small victory against pain and disability, was a testament to my will to live. The hardest part was not my suffering; it was watching my family suffer with me. My children's confusion

BEYOND LIMITS

and their fear of the man I had become broke my heart more than any physical pain ever could.

***

I purchased my very first bike while I was in the military. I had no idea what I was doing, but I wanted it. The thrill of owning a motorcycle was too enticing to resist, so I dove in headfirst. To learn the ropes, I turned to YouTube, absorbing every video I could find about riding techniques and shifting gears. Armed with this newfound knowledge, I took my motorcycle to various parking lots and taught myself how to ride, practicing turns, stops, and starts with relentless determination.

Each session in those empty lots felt like a small victory, building my confidence bit by bit. The sense of freedom and exhilaration I felt as I mastered the basics was incomparable. Once I felt ready, I took the plunge and rode on the highway. The rush of wind, the open road, and the hum of the engine beneath me made all the effort worthwhile. I cherished every moment on that bike, exploring new places and pushing my limits.

For as long as I could, I reveled in the joy of riding. Unfortunately, one day, I found my beloved bike lying in a parking lot, completely totaled after someone had run over it. The sight of it, mangled and lifeless, broke my heart. It felt like losing a trusted companion, one that had carried me through countless adventures and given me a taste of true freedom.

Terrifying enough, lying on the bed in the ICU brought back that familiar pain and dread. This time, though, it wasn't just a machine of metal parts and chassis that had been mangled and lost—it was my body. I faced the terrifying uncertainty of whether I would ever regain what I once had. The bike had been a piece of my freedom, a symbol of my resilience, but now, it was my very self, my physical being, which hung in the balance. The stakes were infinitely higher, and there are a few things that match the fear of not being able to reclaim one's former self; very few things compare to the feeling of a loss so profound and could be more personal and heart-wrenching.

It was another of the many battles that came as a consequence of surviving. That bike I cherished so much never did return to what it was; it was never better. I remember its ending vaguely, largely because it wasn't a part of it I really wanted to remember. In the wake of the excruciating pain in the ICU, after I had grown conscious of myself, this fear was there all along, regardless of what the doctors had told me to expect of my recovery. It was inevitably compounded by the moment my toddler declared he could no longer recognize me.

So, with every day of therapy, I showed up with a mixture of emotions and a multitude of reasons to change my status quo. I wasn't the man who gave up easily; I had proven that time and time again, and this was one more challenge for me to overcome. I needed to prove that my triumph against death was no fluke; I needed my kids to see me again for my family and friends to be more than just glad that I was not dead.

If I were never to be the same man again, and it seemed surely that I wasn't, then I had no choice but to become someone even better than what I had lost in that accident. I needed to dust off the pieces that had broken away and rebuild myself with every milestone since I crawled out of the dirt and escaped my death in the woods along the highway. Each day of therapy was a battle, not just against physical limitations but against the fear and doubt that threatened to undermine my spirit.

I wanted my children to look at me with pride, not pity. I wanted my wife to see in my eyes the determination that first drew us together. I wanted to prove to myself that I could rise from this tragedy, stronger and more resilient, despite what fate had cast for me. I wanted to reclaim my life, to be more than just a man who had survived, one who existed after not dying that day. For anyone else, dare I say even the version of me that lived in an alternate universe, the stakes could never be this high because my life before the accident was filled with so much energy, vigor, and drive for adventure that merely being able to talk, walk and use my hands again would not be enough.

So, while I had been told my estimated time of recovery, a part of me already knew that the physicians had not considered my active lifestyle, which made me. It meant that recovery would likely be longer and more grueling, but with every small victory, I felt a step closer to reclaiming my life. The grander victory was always on my mind, even if it seemed distant.

I understood my journey wouldn't fit neatly into the timelines the doctors provided. They couldn't fully grasp the drive that pushed me to exceed my limits constantly. Every stretch, every lift, and every painful repetition was a reminder of who I was and who I wanted to become again. Each day in therapy, I approached with the same determination that had carried me through countless challenges before—both on and off the battlefield.

BEYOND LIMITS

Chapter Eleven

Imagine sitting on a two-wheeled machine, hands gripping the handlebars. Your first instinct is balance—to stay upright because, despite its incredible power, this machine still depends on you. From balance, you move on to control. The engine starts, it revs, and the hum of the beast awakens every dormant sense within you, firing your neurons into action. You turn the handlebars and throttle the beast, taming it before take-off. It's an incredible feeling.

It doesn't end there. You release the brake and set the beast loose. It fires along whatever path you choose. The asphalt becomes your gateway to an otherworldly experience as you speed along. The tires spin at thousands of revolutions per minute, the wind strikes your face endlessly, and the world blurs behind you. With every tilt, every bend, and every turn, your heart beats so fast it might leap out of your chest, yearning to be free as well, to experience the thrill of freedom even as it pumps into oblivion.

Carmelo Rodriguez

The sensation is electric. The connection between man and machine is symbiotic; the bike responds to your slightest touch, an extension of your will. The roar of the engine is your soundtrack, a constant reminder of the raw power at your command. You lean into a curve, feeling the g-force tug at your body, the tires gripping the road with a tenacity that mirrors your determination.

The straightaways are where you unleash the full potential of the machine, accelerating with a force that presses you into the seat. The landscape whips past in a dizzying blur, the boundary between reality and the dreamlike state of pure speed becoming indistinguishable. The thrill is intoxicating, each second a rush of adrenaline that drowns out all other thoughts and worries.

In a moment like this, you are truly alive, connected to the world in a way that only speed and the open road can provide. The freedom is absolute, the experience transcendent. Every ride is a journey into the sublime, where you leave behind the mundane and embrace the extraordinary.

Trees, buildings, cars, and people blur swiftly into hazy streaks in your periphery. After you've seen them, they disappear into the background, and the world feels unbearably slow. You've discovered something more—like reaching the peak of your speed while everything else crawls at a snail's pace. The roar of the beast beneath you fuels your drive, its smoothness matching the thrill. You wonder why you haven't done this more often.

BEYOND LIMITS

Maybe you have—it might not be your first time hurtling forward at breakneck speed, but each experience feels uniquely exhilarating. Your muscles remember, your neurons fire in familiar patterns, but the adrenaline rush makes it feel refreshingly new every time. Taming a beast like this means knowing when to slow down and when to let loose. It means visualizing the turn before it comes and moving your body instinctively because the bike extends you. Every tilt, every turn, every bend, and every brake maneuver synchronizes with the surge of excitement you feel. It's heavenly, and you know it.

All of this happens when it's just you and your machine alone on the road, nothing to contest your dominance. When you up the ante, the adrenaline spikes to a new level. It's intoxicating. It's dangerous. The stakes are higher, and the thrill is even more intense. Racing against others or pushing your limits on a challenging track, the blend of speed and skill required keeps you on the edge. The danger amplifies the excitement, making every second more vivid, every sensation more acute.

Now, you're not just riding; you're living on the edge of control and chaos, balancing the raw power of the machine with your precision and reflexes. It's a dance with danger, a flirtation with the limits of what's possible. Every time you emerge victorious, you're reminded why you chase this feeling. It's not just about speed; it's about freedom, mastery, and the undeniable rush of being alive.

Carmelo Rodriguez

If you're someone who doesn't like to lose, it might be best to stay away, especially if riding isn't your strong suit. The noise—the cheers and jeers—will get to you one way or another. Either you're amped by it, or it simply gets in your head. Now, picture yourself during all the thrills you've envisioned; only this time, you have a mission. The goal is to amplify the adrenaline with the thrill of victory, going head-to-head, beast-for-beast, against other riders and leaving them in the dust.

Stay with me. Imagine going eighty miles per hour, your heartbeat synced with the rhythm of the race. Every second, you're acutely aware of the bike in front of you and the one on your tail. There's no room to slow down—doing so means you'll be the one eating dust. By nature, humans are competitive. You don't want the rider ahead of you to reach the finish line first. You know you've got a little more in the tank—not just in the beast you're riding, but within yourself. There's a reserve in your drive, in your spirit, and you cautiously tap into it just after the bend, inching closer to the lead.

They may see you, or they may not. It doesn't matter. In the final moments of the race, it's you and your beast that jet past the finish line first. The exhilaration is unmatched. You feel every fiber of your being aligned with the machine beneath you, pushing the limits, defying the odds. The roar of the crowd, the handful of them that's gathered to witness or partake, the wind in your face, the blur of the world around you—all culminate in a single, triumphant moment. You've done it. You've not only conquered the road but also the competition. The taste of victory is sweet, the adrenaline coursing through your veins is unmatched, and there isn't a lot that can be compared to the thrill of the ride. In that moment, perhaps, nothing can even come close.

When you come out on the other end victorious, you've not just raced; you're living fully, embracing the rush of victory and the intense satisfaction of knowing you and your machine have outperformed all others. It's a heady mix of skill, bravery, and sheer determination. As you slow down, the world gradually comes back into focus; you can't deny that you're already thinking about the next race, the next thrill, the next chance to push yourself to the limit once again.

After the disappointment of losing my first bike, I bought a smaller, less powerful model. My goal was to learn stunts and tricks, hoping this new direction would reignite my passion. However, it didn't take long for boredom to set in. The thrill of speed and the rush of adrenaline were missing, and I yearned for fast bikes again.

Determined to recapture that exhilarating feeling, I moved on to my third bike—a Z1000 Kawasaki, the fastest bike I'd ever owned. This bike wasn't just about speed; it became a symbol of my desire to push boundaries. I dove headfirst into the world of street racing and track racing.

For a while, my life revolved around the intense, high-octane world of racing. Late nights and early mornings were spent tweaking my bike, practicing maneuvers, and strategizing for upcoming races.

Carmelo Rodriguez

The sense of community among racers was palpable; we shared a mutual understanding of the risks and rewards of our sport.

The thrill of tearing down the track, the roar of the engine in my ears, and the sheer adrenaline rush as I edged past competitors, made this one of the wildest periods of my life. Each race was a blend of skill, bravery, and a touch of recklessness, and I relished every moment. This chapter of my life was marked by speed, camaraderie, and a constant chase for that next high, always striving to outdo my last performance.

I never really gave much thought to letting go of riding, but I knew that at some point, the thrill would have to come from something else. The essence of a thrill lies in its rarity that it doesn't happen to everyon0065 all the time. If it went on and on without pause, its very point would be lost. Scientists refer to this phenomenon as "tetany" in the study of human physiology—the science of how the human body functions. Tetany is a persistent state of muscle excitation, where the muscles of the body are continuously active and cannot relax.

One might question if it's contradictory to live life hunting for thrills only to anticipate their end. The truth is, the perfect life, if such a thing exists, requires balance. There's no life for someone who drifts through their days without some form of excitement. Yet, on the other end of the scale, a person must recognize when the thrill must be tempered and a descent from the high is necessary. Failing to understand this balance can be disastrous.

BEYOND LIMITS

Much like running nonstop or working without a break, tetany and a ceaseless flood of adrenaline can lead to exhaustion or even death. No matter how euphoric the high feels, there comes a time when it transitions from an escape to a burden. The beauty of the thrill is often found in its absence because it's in that return that we truly appreciate it.

The thrill of riding motorcycles taught me about this delicate balance. The adrenaline rush, the sense of freedom, and the exhilaration were unparalleled, but stepping away made me value those moments even more. When I returned to riding, it wasn't just about chasing the high; it was about savoring it, knowing it wouldn't last forever. This understanding made every ride more meaningful, every victory sweeter, and every quiet moment in between more peaceful.

Life is a series of peaks and valleys. The thrill is the peak, but we need the valleys to rest, reflect, and prepare for the next ascent. This rhythm makes the highs so intoxicating and the returns so anticipated. It's not about abandoning the pursuit of excitement but recognizing its place within the broader tapestry of life. Sometimes, even, we trade some highs for others, and that happened when I realized that I was going to be a father.

***

Learning that I was going to be a dad didn't take away from the excitement of my life; if anything, it compounded it. I don't know which part of me was more excited when I got the news—the adventurer who craved thrills or the man who loved my wife so dearly that I looked forward to realizing our dreams together. They were both me, and the notion of becoming a father started me on a different course with a new source of thrill.

From the day I found out, I was in a persistent state of delight, not one as intense as to cause tetany, but with the thought of my unborn child constantly at the back of my mind. The thrill I derived from riding and street racing was compensated by simply knowing that there was going to be another human being in this life who would share everything about me and my wife, including our love. The endless experiences and the countless memories we were going to create together filled me with dreamy anticipation. The closer the day of meeting our newborn approached, the more excited I became, and the easier it was to realize that the daring and daredevil quests had to end.

I want to make it clear that stepping away from riding when we were expecting a child does not take anything away from my dear wife. It does not imply for even a moment that I didn't value our companionship enough to "play it safe." She was fully aware of the kind of man I was. She was and still is my greatest cheerleader, but the notion of welcoming another life together bore a responsibility that couldn't be matched.

The adventure of fatherhood presented a new kind of thrill—one that didn't involve high speeds or daring stunts but was just as exhilarating. Holding my child for the first time, hearing their first

BEYOND LIMITS

laugh, watching them take their first steps, these moments offered a different kind of rush, a deeper sense of fulfillment. They were milestones that made every sacrifice worthwhile.

In this new chapter, life's excitement took on a unique form. It was much more than the adrenaline-fueled races. The shared journey of raising a child had come into the mix, along with the everyday adventures of parenthood and the joy of watching our family grow. The thrill was still there, but it was now intertwined with a profound sense of purpose and love, and it was worth it.

Becoming a parent was everything I had imagined and more. The overwhelming joy and vulnerability I felt when I first held my child, seeing those tender eyes gaze at me, left an indelible mark on my heart. As the years passed, parenting became an integral part of my life's adventure. Yet, alongside the responsibilities of fatherhood, the urge to ride motorcycles gradually resurfaced.

The thrill, freedom, and connection with the open road called out to me once again to rekindle my passion for motorcycles. I started small, which was when I purchased the cruiser and transformed it into a sleek bobber after pouring countless hours into the project. With the bobber, seeing my vision come to life brought a deep sense of fulfillment, and riding it reignited my love for motorcycles in a way that blended seamlessly with my green, yet the profound experience of parenthood.

Realizing that milestone in my life opened me up for the next one; I'd found a way to return to riding after becoming a father without having to trade one love for the other, and it seemed only right to up the ante once more, which is where the dream of owning a Harley comes in.

The allure of a Harley-Davidson, with its iconic design and powerful performance, had always been at the back of my mind. There's something about the roar of a Harley engine, the craftsmanship, and the sense of heritage that comes with it. It's more than just a bike; it's a symbol of freedom and rebellion, a testament to the spirit of adventure.

Now, as I look into the future, I know that one day, I will make that dream a reality. The bobber was a steppingstone, a reminder of the joy of riding, but the Harley was the goal. It represents not just a return to my passion but an evolution of it. It's about embracing the journey, celebrating the milestones, and looking forward to the rides yet to come.

***

Each person's journey through life is as unique as a fingerprint, and the reasons for choosing any path are as diverse as humanity itself. The allure of riding a motorcycle is no exception to this rule. While countless motivations exist for bikers, they typically fall into one of two broad categories: escape or pursuit. Some seek the open road to break free from the constraints of daily life or something more, while others chase elusive dreams and ambitions.

BEYOND LIMITS

Ask any rider why they choose to mount a motorcycle, and you'll likely get an earful of passionate stories of freedom that can only be felt astride a motorcycle—where the wind whispers secrets of liberation that no other vehicle can offer. They might confess to a craving for the adrenaline rush, the thrill of going as fast as possible, of pushing limits, and cheating death.

In my journey, I've been fortunate to taste both essences.

When I rode, it was with my heart. Every moment was a convergence of my deepest passion and commitment, where hesitation found no place. It was more than a thrill; it was a harmony of skill and heart, an immersion into the very essence of being alive. Riding at that edge was both a challenge and a sanctuary—a place where my complete self could exist without reserve.

Passion doesn't come easy, and perhaps that's why some never fully commit to it while others don't possess it at all. To be driven by something so profound that it propels you to a dreamlike state isn't a luxury everyone can afford. Only those who have found it can truly testify to its immense fulfillment. Passion transcends mere interest or participation; it's about being completely consumed by something that demands your full attention and heart. Anything less than total dedication means it's no longer passion.

My commitment to riding was absolute; nothing was lacking. Every moment on the bike was a convergence of my deepest passion and commitment, where hesitation found no place. It was more than a thrill; it was a symphony of skill and emotion, an immersion into the very essence of being alive. Riding at the edge was both a challenge and a sanctuary—a space where my entire self could exist without reserve.

This intense dedication carried over to my subsequent adventures and passions. Whether it was my military service, my career as a stuntman, or my journey as a writer, I did everything with the same unwavering commitment. The famous saying, "Whatever is worth doing at all is worth doing well," stuck deeply with me. Each endeavor claimed a part of my life, and each received the right portion of attention to sustain it and keep it from becoming dangerous.

I've come to understand that nothing poses a greater peril than a passion left unfulfilled or half-hearted. It's a dangerous illusion, deceiving those who carry it into believing they are fully engaged when, in truth, they are not. This incomplete passion not only jeopardizes personal endeavors but also casts a shadow over everything and everyone around. It fosters false confidence that can lead to recklessness, endangering not just our way of life but life itself.

When passion lacks depth, it opens the door to poor decisions born of naivety rather than wisdom—stupidity, to put it bluntly. In such cases, the absence of wholehearted commitment leaves us vulnerable, exposing us to risks we may not fully comprehend.

BEYOND LIMITS

Passion, when nurtured and embraced completely, becomes a force for clarity and purpose, something that guides us toward decisions rooted in experience rather than uncertainty.

A half-hearted passion is as precarious as a broken chain holding one aloft a thousand feet in the air. It creates a spectacle suspended in the air for the world to see, yet it is moments away from disaster. Without the grounding force of full commitment, we are left vulnerable, our endeavors fragile, and our confidence false.

Fully embracing passion transforms it into a powerful force for good. It provides clarity, drives purpose, and ensures that our decisions are made with wisdom and experience. It gives a total commitment to passion; they safeguard themselves against the dangers of naivety and half-heartedness.

With prolonged therapy ahead of me, I must face this challenge with unwavering determination. Surviving my ordeal was a significant achievement, but now, my goal extends beyond mere survival—I aim to live truly. Despite the formidable obstacles that lie ahead, I am committed to transforming this journey into a new passion.

There's a common saying that some great individuals are defined by the events that happen to them. However, fate doesn't deserve all the credit; each person has choices to make. In every scenario, no matter how impossible or daunting the odds, there is always an option: to fight or surrender, to hold on or let go, to be present, or to withdraw. Often, stories focus on the survivors and overlook those who made critical decisions on their behalf.

I am quite aware that my survival is not solely my accomplishment. It is the result of the collective support from those around me who stood by me during the hardest times, even when I was likely insufferable. From concerned strangers to dedicated medical professionals, from friends and family to my unwavering wife, I owe my life to those who made me their priority. Their compassion and commitment became my lifeline, and my wife's steadfast support was my anchor. I would not be without those who considered me their passion, and I was always hers.

Chapter Twelve

When life presents us with choices, we can only hope that we make the right one. Often, the results aren't immediate or obvious; sometimes, it takes nearly a lifetime to understand their impact fully. By then, time might no longer be on our side, leaving little room for a do-over. Sometimes, we don't grasp the gravity of our choices until life hands us a reality far from the perfect picture scene we once imagined. We're left lamenting past decisions amidst present anguish.

One of the most significant choices in life is selecting a partner, and I do not doubt that I made the absolute best choice I could have.

While my consciousness was subdued by pain during my time in the ICU, Diana was a constant presence by my side. Her importance in my life cannot be overstated. She was there before the accident, and in the fleeting moments of clarity after being hurtled across the I-95, she was the first person I thought of, along with our children. It was her face I yearned to see and her voice I desperately wanted to hear. She was the one person in the universe that mattered to me, the one I wanted a last moment with if that ride in the ambulance was going to be my last.

Before the accident, my life wasn't perfect. I loved my wife and my family deeply, but like every other relationship, there were hurdles we needed to overcome. Our life wasn't without its challenges. This didn't diminish our affection for each other, but I might have been a little carried away with my responsibilities. We were navigating the complexities of balancing careers, parenthood, and our relationship. There were moments of frustration and distance as I struggled to juggle my numerous roles while being a devoted husband and father.

Although I am not one to give fate credit for every little thing that goes wrong in my life, my relationship with Diana took a turn after the accident that I doubt would have happened otherwise. The trials of my recent motorcycle accident made me realize how pivotal my choice was. Diana has always been a devoted partner, even when I wasn't conscious of it; she supported me and my plans and dreams in ways that I would only discover later. Yet, a series of challenges was taking a toil on our family. Then the incident happened, and nothing else mattered. The only thing I cared about was surviving so I could see her again and let her know just how much she meant to me and how deeply I loved her.

In the wake of my admission to the ICU and the revelation that I was practically living in a suspended state with one foot in this realm and the other in a realm beyond reach, Diana never left my side. I did not need to be told; even in my barely conscious state, she was the warmth and the tether that cushioned me to hang on and find my way back. The poetry of her hand holding mine when I woke will never be lost to me. It is only because of her I'm not alone.

As the days passed, I became increasingly aware of her constant presence. My wife spent almost every night in the hospital with me, even after the medical staff told her she couldn't stay. Her argument was simple and resolute, "I almost lost him once. I'm not doing that again."

Diana's determination was an invaluable show of her love and commitment. She defied the hospital's rules, staying by my side and holding my hand so I would know that I wasn't alone. Each night, as the world outside continued, my steadfast companion remained next to me, ensuring I never felt abandoned. Her presence was more than comforting; it was life-affirming. In those moments of pain and uncertainty, Diana was my anchor, grounding me and giving me the strength to keep fighting. Her face was the first thing I saw when I opened my eyes, and her voice was the melody that soothed my fears.

As profound as her statement was to everyone she told, it hit a little harder for me because, before this motorcycle accident, we were going through our difficulties. This accident forced me to sit down and figure out what's important: family. Diana's unwavering presence during my recovery has been a stark reminder of the strength of our bond. The accident forced me to reassess my priorities and realize how much I had taken for granted. Her resilience and love have been my lifeline, showing me that amid all the chaos, she is my constant, my anchor, and my greatest support.

In my decades of existence, I've made choices that have marked my life, in one way or the other, along the way. It is often difficult to think of the little choices one makes that lead up to bigger ones. Still, the turn my life took, and my tango with death had me pondering on those seemingly inconsequential ones, like my decision to step out of the house the day I met Diana or the tilt of my head that brought her to my sight. I have forever been indebted to those, as only with them was I able to make the greatest choice of my life—marrying her.

***

I spent many years in the military and law enforcement, where I gained a unique skill set and extensive experience. There's no denying that when I transitioned to the film industry, finding gigs that revolved around these careers came naturally. Once I started marketing myself within those parameters, I began as an extra in films. By highlighting my background and skill levels, I quickly moved into background work and eventually found my niche in stunt work.

Then, I was eventually told that to land bigger contracts; I needed formal education in the field, call it a foolproof way to ensure that I wasn't in it with half a passion. I attended a school in the Maryland area, and I learned some very invaluable lessons. This education allowed me to market myself as a well-rounded stuntman with specialized training. I trained as a bodyguard, honed my skills in precision driving, and dedicated significant time to martial arts. Additionally, I gained knowledge of medical response and firearms expertise. These capabilities made me a versatile asset in Hollywood, where such skills are highly sought after.

My latest stunt work primarily involved fight scenes, raids, and shootouts. I have also done small commercials, demonstrated workout routines, and lifted weights for social media businesses. For a while, I was training to fly airplanes to add that to my résumé. However, after my accident, I became disqualified because of the medication I now take.

There's something about experiencing trauma that affects you in ways you might not even be conscious of. I might have been an adventurer before the military, but there's a part of me that wonders if the paths I chose afterward were all in line with merely making a living with what I knew or if, secretly, they were careers to mask the horror I faced in the military, the things I could never really deal with.

Reflecting on my journey, I realize that my choices were influenced by a desire to stay within my comfort zone using my skills to build a new career. The transition from military and law enforcement to stunt work allowed me to continue working in high-adrenaline environments, where my training was not only relevant but also highly valued. The structured chaos of film sets, the precision required in stunt work, and the camaraderie among the crew provided a sense of familiarity and purpose that helped me navigate the complexities of civilian life.

Each role I took on each scene I performed was a step toward healing, even if I didn't fully recognize it at the time. The discipline, focus, and resilience I developed in the military became my greatest assets in the film industry. Through my work, I channeled my experiences into something creative and fulfilling, turning what could have been a burden into a source of strength and pride.

Maybe there's an argument to be made that I am an overachiever, never content with being average. Everything I do is approached with such commitment that anything less feels like a sin. From my military days, where I believed I was the most eager to ensure mission success, to my passion for biking, to my career as a versatile stuntman, I have always pushed beyond the norm. Limits were never something I was comfortable with, not if I could help it.

This relentless drive has shaped my journey. In the military, I was determined to excel to be the best I could be for my team and my

BEYOND LIMITS

country. The discipline and resilience I developed there carried over into my civilian life. When I transitioned to stunt work, I brought the same level of dedication and intensity. I refused to be just a stuntman; I trained in multiple disciplines, becoming skilled in bodyguard work, precision driving, martial arts, medical response, and firearms. My goal was to be as versatile as possible to bring something unique and invaluable to every role.

The desire to break free from limitations was also what propelled me out of the death-induced haze in the forest after my accident. In those moments of pain and near despair, my longing to see my wife and family again was intertwined with a deeper, almost primal drive. I wanted to stand proud, to face death and emerge triumphant.

I can't deny that besides wanting to live for my loved ones, there was also a part of me that yearned to conquer the ultimate challenge, to look back and say, "I faced death and won." This drive, this refusal to accept limits, has been a constant in my life. It's what pushed me through the toughest times and what continues to motivate me to this day.

In every aspect of my life, from military missions to film sets, I have strived to give my best. The idea of settling for less is foreign to me. This mentality has not only defined my career but also my approach to life. Whether it's performing stunts, training in new skills, or simply being there for my family, I aim to do it all with unwavering commitment and passion.

Carmelo Rodriguez

This journey has taught me that while pushing boundaries can be demanding, it also brings immense fulfillment. It's about challenging myself, embracing every opportunity to grow, and never settling for mediocrity.

Fast forward through the grueling recovery and therapy, and I found myself, once again, seeking the overachiever within me. I needed that relentless spirit to propel me through the tough days and help me regain the person I was before the accident.

In a journey that was guaranteed to be far from easy, each day brought new challenges, from regaining physical strength to overcoming mental hurdles, but if there was one thing I knew how to do, it was how to stay locked on when I found it purposeful. Like calling on a god within me, I had to channel the same drive that had pushed me to excel in the military and law enforcement, the same commitment that had made me a versatile stuntman. I went into every day of my recovery with the same intensity, refusing to let myself to defined with limitations that never stopped threatening.

Physical therapy sessions became missions to accomplish, with each small victory a step closer to reclaiming my life. Apart from my family, I drew strength from my past, remembering the discipline and resilience that had seen me through countless trials and other tough times. Days were filled with exercises, stretches, and treatments that were going to rebuild my body, while my

BEYOND LIMITS

nights were spent visualizing my goals and reminding myself of why I was fighting so hard.

Beyond the physical aspects, there was also a deep emotional and psychological journey. As surely the accident had forced me to confront my vulnerabilities and reassess what truly mattered. I leaned heavily on the support of my wife, whose solid presence was a constant source of motivation for me. Her belief in me fuelled my determination to push through the pain and fatigue.

It might have seemed bleak at first, but as days passed, I saw glimpses of the old me—the overachiever who never backed down from a challenge. It was a crucial part of my identity that was returning slowly but surely. The people who surrounded me, the therapists and my family, made it easier, as I was often immersed in activities that brightened me up and gave me purpose. The desire to come back, to be more than just a survivor, drove me forward.

One finger after the other, one step after another, each day, I felt a little stronger, a little more like myself. The journey was far from over, but I was on the right path. Having faced the biggest challenge of my life, switching to the overachiever in me was the only way I could be sure that I stood a chance of coming out on the other side.

Carmelo Rodriguez

Chapter Thirteen

As days melted seamlessly into nights, the distinction between them vanished, and our mission objectives shifted as our intel grew increasingly outdated. It had been days since we embarked on the rescue mission for our comrades, victims of a brutal ambush. The relentless search for the enemy's hideout, where we believed survivors might be held hostage, was proving futile. It was hard not to feel dispirited as we thought of our comrades, who could still be alive, clinging to hope and waiting for our help. Each soldier among us was an extension of ourselves, someone we could never abandon.

The intel we had was vague and unreliable. It promised nothing except the grim fact that the ambush had claimed several of our comrades, whose bodies were used as traps to capture more of us. For such a large-scale ambush, it seemed impossible that we couldn't locate a single hideout where the insurgents might be hiding. Despite our trust in the intel source, doubts crept in. Were we on a wild goose chase? Had we been misled? These questions haunted us, yet we pressed on, driven by an untiring determination to find our brothers-in-arms.

Regardless of the intel's credibility, caution was always our instinctive response. In war, loyalties could shift without warning. Allies could become enemies in an instant, willing to betray us to save their own lives. You can only hope that you learn this before they approach and point you in a direction that feeds on your desperation. The mission was tense with peril and uncertainty, but there could be no hesitation because the bond between us soldiers remained unbreakable. We continued our search, propelled by the unyielding belief that we must save those who were an integral part of our unit, our family.

As the hours of the mission grew increasingly futile, doubts about the accuracy of the intel intensified. If it hadn't been compromised, then the grim reality of our captured comrades' fate loomed large in our minds. Each passing second made it harder to avoid imagining the worst, but we couldn't afford to entertain such thoughts. It was crucial to maintain our fighting spirit. Despite knowing the enemy's brutality and savagery, we kept reminding ourselves that until proven otherwise, our brothers were still out there, waiting for us to rescue them.

We trudged on relentlessly, combing through camps, villages, and towns, both from the air and on foot. The insurgents' footprints were unmistakable, visible even from a thousand feet in the air. The devastation they left in their wake was a constant reminder of the horror they spread, enough to instill fear in ordinary men. We encountered this terror at every turn, each mission revealing more of the enemy's cruelty and the harsh reality our comrades might be facing.

The terrain we navigated was far from forgiving; each landscape was a silent witness to the chaos and destruction wrought by the insurgents, yet we moved with determination. Every piece of evidence, every sign of life, was meticulously examined, fueling our hope that we were getting closer. The villages we passed through bore the scars of conflict, their inhabitants often too terrified to speak, yet their eyes held silent pleas for justice and peace.

Our search extended into the night, with the darkness adding another layer of danger. The flickering lights from distant fires painted a haunting picture of the land ravaged by war. We relied on each other, drawing strength from the unspoken bond that united us. The weight of our mission was heavy, but the thought of our comrades enduring unimaginable suffering kept us moving forward.

To think that it was people we knew who had been ambushed made us restless, robbing me of sleep for several nights. It could very well have been us if our paths had been different. That was one of the most terrifying aspects of war: the unpredictability. One moment, you could be safe in your camp, plotting a mission to advance on the enemy, and the next, you're walking into a trap meticulously designed with you in mind. One second, you're knee-deep in the dirt, sharing jokes to lift the spirits among the ranks, setting up an ambush for enemy combatants, and the next, you're exchanging fire so rapidly you can barely hear yourself think over the gunfire.

The unpredictability of war was a constant shadow, looming over every decision and movement. The thought that our comrades, people we shared meals with, trained with, and considered brothers, had been caught in such a deadly snare was a gnawing pain. It was a grim reminder of how thin the line was between life and death on the battlefield. The randomness of survival haunted us all, making every step we took feel like a step closer to the unknown.

The laughter we shared to keep morale high felt like a distant memory amidst the cacophony of gunfire. The soldier who had laughed at my joke moments before now lay lifeless a few yards away, his blood soaking into the ground. The stark contrast between those fleeting moments of camaraderie and the brutal reality of combat was jarring. It underscored the fragility of our existence, how quickly things could change, and how powerless we were to stop it.

There are no guarantees in life and war, even less so. Therefore, anyone brave enough to answer their country's call to serve and defend deserves every ounce of respect they receive. They make a conscious decision, fully aware that they might embark on a mission and never return. They put their lives on the line to fight when most would rather not.

The unpredictability of war, with its constant threat of sudden violence and loss, underscores the deep courage it takes to step onto the battlefield. Those who serve do so with the understanding that each day could be their last, yet they choose to stand firm, driven by a sense of duty and honor. This willingness to face the unknown, to confront fear and danger head-on, is proof of their strength and character.

To serve in the military is to accept the harsh reality that safety is a fleeting notion, and the next moment could bring anything from camaraderie to chaos. It is a path marked by sacrifice, where personal safety is very often traded for the greater good. This selflessness, this readiness to defend and protect, even at the risk of one's own life, is what makes the service so commendable.

Faced with war's brutal unpredictability, soldiers forge bonds that are deeper than friendship. These bonds are born from shared experiences of hardship and danger, and they create a brotherhood that transcends the battlefield. We fight not just for our country but for each other, each act of bravery a reflection of our unshakeable commitment to those by their side.

Respect for these brave individuals is not just about honoring their service but also recognizing the sacrifices they make. It's about acknowledging the weight of the burdens they carry, the physical and emotional scars they endure, and the tireless spirit they embody. Their courage and dedication are a beacon of hope and resilience, a reminder of the extraordinary things ordinary people can achieve in the face of adversity.

Every soldier, every person who dons the uniform, carries with them the stories of those who came before and those who will come after. They are part of a legacy of bravery and sacrifice, a lineage of individuals who understood the true cost of freedom and paid it willingly. This legacy is a powerful testament to the human spirit's capacity for courage and selflessness, deserving of the highest respect and gratitude.

Finding a soldier who's been lost in the hands of the enemy is an unmatched feeling. It's so rare that it's often considered an act of the Divine. We hoped for this. Even after learning that some had died and others were used as cannon fodder, we hoped for a miracle. A few days later, after all the efforts, the search led to the Tigris River, where we would realize that acts of Divine might as well be myths.

The heartbreak began several miles away, growing heavier with each meter as we approached, the stench of death creeping in long before we saw anything. There's something about silence that, on its own, becomes an unfiltered terror, especially when it descends so suddenly. It's the kind of silence that chills you to the bone when you approach a location where your comrades, missing for days, should be. A place exposed and desolate, where nothing that seeks to survive in the middle of an embattled territory would loiter.

From the stench and crippling silence, we descended fully upon our arrival at the riverbank, where the last shred of naïve hope among us dissolved. Figures dotted the surface of the black water, lumps with hands and feet splayed out. Heartbreak, which had begun miles away, now sent chills down my spine and those of my comrades as we stood there, witnessing the headless bodies of our friends floating in the river.

These weren't just soldiers; they were people we knew, people we had laughed with and shared stories with. The sight was devastating, a brutal end to the hope we had clung to. Each face, now gone, flashed in my memory, making the scene before us more personal and gut-wrenching. The river, which once might have been a symbol of life, was a solitary and silent witness to their final, horrific moments.

Even now, I find myself questioning how I managed to stand tall despite the paralyzing rage that consumed me when we recovered the corpses of my fellow soldiers, their heads, and other body parts missing. I remember the overwhelming desire for retaliation that filled me then.

Days passed, and we located a few more—what was left of them. The mission to recover our missing soldiers was yielding, albeit it was the last way we hoped we would find any of them. The numbers increased with time, but we never found them all. There was no Divine act. To this day, the search continues, a constant lookout for the remaining.

To grasp just how cruel the world is and how much of a savage the enemy we faced was, there was talk of video footage that was published as the soldiers were beheaded. The mere thought of it intensified my rage as it broke my heart, even though I never cared to see it because I couldn't watch that be the end of my comrades and friends.

Sergeant Hernandez was more than just a fellow soldier; he was a part of my community. Back home, we gathered with our families and had cookouts. I considered him more of a brother and friend than a colleague. I knew his family and shared his stories, but I had to return with the devastating news that he never made it. I couldn't bring myself to recount the gruesome details of his end to anyone. I prefer to remember him as the brother with whom I fought and shared good times, along with our families.

***

One of the profound challenges of human existence is the persistent discord between our physical selves and our mental and emotional states. This dissonance often goes unnoticed, relegated to the background until moments when our bodies falter, failing to align with our inner resolve and aspirations. It's a profound sense of betrayal—a stark reminder that physical limitations can undermine our willpower and spirit.

One aspect of resilience is summoning the courage to persevere despite these discrepancies. However, the true test lies in navigating life's battles when our bodies refuse to cooperate with the decisions our minds have made. While it's natural for the mind to guide the body, severe trauma can disrupt this synchrony, leaving us adrift from our intended path.

In moments like that, the rhythm of existence falters, and the journey back to alignment with our true selves becomes a daunting challenge. It's a reminder that our journey through life is not just about overcoming external obstacles but also about reconciling the internal discord that can arise when our physical and mental realms clash.

This phenomenon differs from the shock that immobilizes the mind, causing the body to hesitate. I've encountered moments where I was so shell-shocked by what I witnessed I couldn't move a muscle momentarily. However, one of the most pivotal moments of my life revealed a profound struggle between my mind and body as I endeavored to heal.

At that critical juncture, I faced an intense internal conflict. My mind was determined to recover, to progress beyond the trauma, yet my body seemed unwilling or unable to keep pace. It was a battle waged deep within me, where the resilience of my spirit clashed against the physical constraints that threatened to hinder my path forward.

BEYOND LIMITS

After coming to terms with the fact that therapy was my best chance to reclaim my life—to become the husband and father my family needed and rediscover my true self, I embraced the encouragement of therapists, family, and friends, as well as the overachiever within me. I was determined to prove that my survival was not just a stroke of luck.

However, amid all the optimism and support, I never expected the moments when my mind would be resolute but my body would falter. Sometimes, I willed myself forward with all the determination I could muster, much like I had done in the past, only to find my physical strength or capabilities insufficient to meet the demands.

The lingering effects of trauma were far from gone despite ongoing treatments and physical therapy. While I hadn't fully recovered physically, several sessions had passed, and despite their grueling nature, I had been left with a glimmer of hope that progress was indeed possible. Then, the next phase of my journey brought a profound new challenge—one that went way beyond physical discomfort.

It felt as though my body was rebelling against every effort I made to move, from the smallest gestures of my fingers and hands to the larger movements of my ankles and legs. It was a disconcerting sensation as if I had awakened in the unfamiliar body of a stranger all over again, like the very first moments after

Carmelo Rodriguez

I regained consciousness in the ICU. I no longer had a connection to the intuitive understanding that once guided my movements.

This experience marked a pivotal moment in my recovery, a stark reminder of the complexities of healing from trauma. It wasn't just about physical rehabilitation anymore; it was about confronting the psychological and emotional barriers that hindered my progress. It demanded a deeper level of resilience and self-discovery, navigating through uncertainty while striving to reconnect with my body and reclaim a sense of familiarity and control.

I couldn't understand it, and even as the therapists tried to explain that sometimes the body can revolt or lock when it's under pressure, I still couldn't comprehend why it was precipitating. This was one of the most significant moments that compounded my frustration in my journey towards recovery. It seemed that all the days I'd shown up had been for nothing. The trembling in my hands increased with every weight, and it seemed my body did not understand the command to do what I wanted, let alone attempt it.

Even with support, as I was helped on the rails to exercise, putting weight on my feet, I couldn't take a single step on my own. It was the peak of frustration, making me wonder if I had deluded myself into thinking that I could get better. I had gone through so much to get to where I was, but it seemed as though, with every challenge I overcame, a different one arose. One would have thought that for someone who escaped death, there should be no deterrent, but it got to me. It took days of giving myself a break and trying to reconnect my body with my overachieving mind before I could finally get back on track.

The frustration was overwhelming. I had faced death and survived, yet here I was, struggling with basic movements. The dissonance between my will and my body's capability was stark and disheartening. It felt as though my efforts were in vain, each small step forward countered by a larger setback. This mental and physical tug-of-war drained me, leaving me questioning my resolve and strength.

During this period, I had to learn patience anew. It wasn't just about pushing through the physical barriers but also about accepting the pace at which my body needed to heal. The process demanded a level of self-compassion I wasn't accustomed to. I had to be kinder to myself, acknowledging that progress isn't always linear and that setbacks are part of the journey.

Gradually, I saw minor improvements. The trembling in my hands lessened, and with time and persistence, I put weight on my feet again. Each tiny victory was a reminder that I was still moving forward, even if it was slower than I had hoped. The support from my therapists, friends, and family became crucial in these moments, providing the encouragement I needed to keep going.

With this, a few things came to mind. First, I realized that the timelines we set for ourselves aren't always realistic. Sometimes, the body and mind need time apart for true healing to occur. This doesn't have to be grand; it could be as simple as a moment of deep meditation and reflection, where no physical activity is demanded of the body. Not just sleep or rest, but a conscious understanding that a biological reset is necessary.

Another realization was how much we underestimate the hold trauma can have on us, even decades later. At the Tigris River, witnessing the atrocity done to my comrades, despite being prepared for the worst, my mind hadn't let go of the will to find my fellow soldiers alive. I wasn't naïve; I hoped that, for once, it wouldn't turn out the way we had feared. Seeing the corpses of my comrades felt like a betrayal of my will, although then it wasn't between my mind and my body.

Years down the line, as I found myself stunted in rehab from an accident unrelated to that traumatic event, a memory of the massacre from over a decade before slid into my mind. I was still clueless about how it surfaced, but it did. This unexpected flashback reminded me of the deep-seated impact of trauma, which can resurface at any moment, influencing our current struggles in profound ways.

This period of introspection taught me the importance of patience and self-compassion. The journey to recovery wasn't just about physical rehabilitation but also about addressing the psychological scars that had been left behind. Trauma isn't a linear experience, and its effects can ripple through our lives in ways we don't immediately understand.

BEYOND LIMITS

Understanding this connection between past trauma and present struggles helped me approach my recovery with a new perspective. I learned to listen to my body, to give it the time and space it needed to heal and to acknowledge the mental battles that were just as significant. The process of healing became more holistic, integrating both physical and emotional recovery.

Reflecting on this experience, I realized that the battle was as much mental as it was physical. My mind's resilience had to match my body's ability to heal. This journey taught me the profound strength that lies in persistence and the importance of celebrating small milestones. Despite the dissonance between my body and mind, I reconnected them, inching closer to recovery each day.

Chapter Fourteen

There aren't many experiences that compare to being thrown from a motorcycle when a vehicle that hit you traveled over 120 miles per hour on the highway. Surviving such an ordeal is nothing short of miraculous. If you do, then every so often, you might find yourself just like I do, reflecting on that moment, marveling at how you cheated death and wondering about the strength that carried you through.

I remember crawling out of the dirt, standing on broken ankles so rescuers could locate me. That moment was just the beginning of an arduous journey. Despite enduring some of the most agonizing pain and challenges, the full account of my penance for defying death remains incomplete.

The aftermath of the accident left me with several injuries that defied comprehension. Aside from over 70% of my body is covered in road burns, with each one treated as a combination of second and third-degree burns, causing excruciating pain that seemed to permeate every inch of my being, even when I was undergoing treatment sessions. The impact had severe internal consequences as well.

My heart shifted from its normal position to proof that the sheer force of the collision had changed my life forever. Every time I recall the doctors saying this, I try to picture it, and it's just beyond my comprehension. It's the first time I've heard someone alive to hear it. The damage extended to my pancreas, which ceased its vital function of producing insulin, requiring immediate medical intervention to manage my blood sugar levels. My spleen sustained partial damage, which required urgent surgery to salvage what could be saved.

Physically, the trauma was devastating. My arm bore the brunt of the impact, shattering into pieces that required metal bars to hold it together. Emergency procedures were performed swiftly on my arm and wrist, preventing the grim prospect of amputation. Meanwhile, the skin on my hands was so severely damaged that muscle and bone were exposed, a testament to the intensity of the road abrasions.

Blood flowed profusely from all my injuries, a stark reminder of the violence of the accident. Even my vocal cords were not spared, sustaining damage that affected my ability to communicate. The force of the impact also ripped out my hair and left my entire body covered in deep bruises, each one a painful reminder of the ordeal I had survived.

Internally, the damage was equally severe. My back was broken in three different places, raising serious concerns about my mobility and ability to walk again. The prospect of rehabilitation seemed daunting, with uncertainty hanging over the extent of my recovery.

Yet, amid the wreckage of my body and spirit, there emerged a glimmer of hope. Supported by the unwavering care of medical professionals and the love of my family, I embarked on a journey of recovery marked by unimaginable challenges and small victories. Each day became evidence of resilience as I fought to reclaim my health, my mobility, and, ultimately, my life.

There are several other injuries I likely do not remember, not necessarily because they were so immaterial to recall, but because there were so many of them that I do not actively keep the record in my head. It is, to where it might be easier to mention which system in my body wasn't affected than the ones that were. To say that it's a miracle I survived wouldn't be overstating it, and considering the milestones of ordeal that followed waking up in the ICU, there surely was still a lot more to do, even after the miracle.

Sometimes, miracles occur unexpectedly, catching us off guard and unprepared. In those moments, if we fail to seize the opportunity, it can feel like a missed chance—a squandered gift of a second lease on life. Not doing everything possible to make that newfound life count is a disservice to oneself.

BEYOND LIMITS

Certainly, sometimes, shock renders us momentarily unable to discern the best course of action or how to react. However, even in those critical moments, our mindset plays a pivotal role. It can be the lifeline that helps us cling on until help arrives or until we can gather our bearings.

When faced with a second chance at life, whether recovering from a traumatic event or overcoming a significant setback, it demands a proactive approach. It requires a commitment to embracing life fully and pursuing goals and aspirations with renewed vigor and determination.

Excuses may arise from disbelief, uncertainty, or fear, but ultimately, our mindset guides us through adversity. It empowers us to channel our resilience and strength, enabling us to navigate challenges and seize opportunities for growth and fulfillment.

Limits are fragile, and once they are shattered, new boundaries emerge in their place. It's a testament to the human experience that we often underestimate our capabilities until we are confronted with the direst circumstances.

When faced squarely with desperate moments, we are pushed beyond what we thought possible. It's in these crucibles of adversity that our true strength and resilience come to light. Whether it's overcoming physical pain, enduring emotional turmoil, or navigating profound challenges, each test of our limits unveils new dimensions of our capacity to persevere and thrive.

Carmelo Rodriguez

I survived the ultimate challenge of my life and lived to tell the tale; one would think that perhaps the ordeal would have been enough to dissuade anyone else from anything related to the object that played a part in the incident. Still, it's far from the case for me.

Biking has never been a fleeting hobby I wanted to explore solely for the sake of the euphoric feeling that came from it or the façade of doing something as unique as being a daredevil. It was a part of my childhood and has been part of my life for as long as I've drawn breath, even when I wasn't actively involved in it—when I wasn't riding because I'd taken a break or didn't get the chance to, it never truly left my mind. A part of my mind wandered with every chance that I got towards the experience, both past and future. It's an interest I couldn't abstain from just because I hadn't ridden in a while.

The mere mention of a motorbike had my mind running pistons about the specs: the make, the model, what kind of power the engine was packing, and how smoothly it ran compared to several others. It's an innate habit that, frankly, might never go away, no matter how much fate tries to taint the memories.

My misadventure on the I-95 had nothing to do with the vehicle I was riding or my handling of it; rather, it stemmed from a reckless, drunk individual who didn't value the lives of road users enough that he pelted along the highway at 120 miles per hour. Regardless of what vehicle it was, whoever the victim was would have suffered to some degree. Knowing that the Harley didn't cause my accident was inconsequential for me because even if it had, bikers embarked on every ride knowing that anything could happen, just like every other road user. The trick to fearlessness is to trust your beast and to ride, even at the best of speeds, to enjoy the freedom of the road, knowing that life is irreplaceable.

So, when I say that despite everything I've been through, with not enough time has passed for me to forget, the hum of a machine or the sight of a two-wheeled beast stirs the memories, I bear no guilt because, as a rider, I'd been thinking of when if ever again I could get back on a bike and feel the freedom of the road fearlessly with the wind against my face when I'd been told I was looking at two years of recovery, a part of me wanted to ask if that was when I could bike again.

The doctors might eventually give me the green light, a date circled in red on some invisible calendar, but cycling was never just about pronouncements and recovery milestones. It was a mark woven from the hum of the engine, the caress of the wind on my face, and the quiet symphony of thoughts echoing in my helmet.

Out there, on the open road, the world shrank to the dance between me and the machine. Every turn demanded a conversation, a negotiation between rider and asphalt. It was a language I spoke fluently, a rhythm etched into my soul. Now, the only rhythm was the relentless beep of the monitor, a stark contrast to the roar of the engine that once filled my dreams.

Would I ever reclaim that language? Would my body ever sing that song again? The questions gnawed at me, a constant undercurrent beneath the ever-present ache.

I was as confused as I was upset. How did I get here? Yes, the literal sequence of events that had seen me catapult off the highway wasn't crystal clear in my head, but something else was missing aside from moments of feeling the knock and opening my eyes in the woods. Was there a turning point, a moment before the crash, that set me on this collision course with disaster? Had I missed a crucial sign, a detour I should have taken on the journey of my life?

What had I done so horribly that led me to this point? Everything I had ever worked for culminated in plans I had set out, but because of a drunk driver, my whole life had come to an almost complete stop.

Suddenly, regardless of the realization of how far I'd come, these questions never left, and they accompanied the tool that worked harder than a string of memories and intense pain.

Now what? The days felt endless, each one dragging on with relentless pain. I felt like I was getting nowhere. I had always been so independent, but now I needed help to wipe my ass. The pain was so intense that I couldn't fall asleep. I couldn't think about anything else except the pain. It got so bad that I asked myself the forbidden question even after braving the odds and coming off the precipice to be celebrated. Why didn't I die? Why couldn't it have been so simple?

Just like the debriding and the therapy, the medications I took were grueling, causing me to lose weight. It seemed that they were making me sicker than I'd ever been. What the hell was wrong with me?

If I had my journal with me, it would sit on the bedside table like a cruel joke. Its pages, once brimming with meticulously planned itineraries and scribbled dreams, now sat blank, a stark reflection of my emptiness. Back then, restless energy thrummed through me, each sunrise an invitation to a new adventure. Now, even the simple act of lifting my head felt like scaling a mountain, the dull ache in my body a constant companion. Those vibrant plans, once the compass guiding me toward a future bursting with possibilities, were now faded memories, overshadowed by a suffocating cloud of pain and despair. Each day stretched before me like a desolate highway, every sunrise a mocking reminder of the journey I could no longer take.

The independence I once took for granted was now a distant dream. The constant reminder that I couldn't do the simplest of tasks without assistance was a realization that perpetually crushed my spirit. It was as if my body had betrayed me, leaving me stranded in a world where every second stretched into an eternity of suffering. I couldn't escape the relentless cycle of pain and medication; each new dose was a reminder of my broken state, no matter how many days had passed.

Sleep should naturally be an escape, but it was no longer a refuge. The pain I felt invaded my dreams, turning them into nightmares. I would wake up drenched in sweat, my body aching even more than before. There was no relief; the moments of respite seemed not to exist. Every breath was a struggle, every heartbeat a painful reminder of the fact that my life had almost been shattered. There was no escape from the thoughts, no matter the "up" sides.

I tried to find solace in the small victories, the moments when I could move without too much pain, or when I managed to eat a full meal. Those moments were fleeting; I had more of the torment that trailed my misadventure and quickly overshadowed my quest to return to who I was before. The relentless march of ache and despair let root thoughts I could not bring myself to repeat in front of my family. It was hard to hold on to hope when every day felt like a battle I was losing.

I used to be someone who faced challenges head-on and took pride in overcoming obstacles. Ever since I was a young man, I took challenges with a heart that I could overcome whatever it was if I tried hard and if I was committed enough. One would think that for a man who had seen war, death, and the cruelty that life could use fate against him, nothing else would faze him, but this felt insurmountable, a never-ending nightmare from which I couldn't wake up. The accident had taken more than just my physical health; it had stolen my sense of self and my identity as a strong person. Now, I was just someone struggling to survive each day, hoping that I could regain some sense of who I used to be before.

I searched for moments of encouragement and positivity, and it eluded me for a long time. Just as my ache was persistent and my torment seemed unending, something else was there; someone else was there. I found moments of clarity when I looked into my wife's eyes. Her support was an abundance of love that seemed so surreal that a part of me wondered if it was all an illusion, a ruse she was playing too well, and maybe she knew something I didn't know and perhaps was being kind while she bid her time for when it would all be over, and I would die. This taboo thought crossed my mind at a point when I almost lost my will to live.

My independence had transformed me into a reliance on Diana. She fed me, bathed me, and cleaned me up. She took care of me as if she were taking care of herself.

In this shared trauma, we created a bond that differed from what we were used to. I relied on her strength, just as she relied on me to stay alive. In those moments, nothing else mattered. I wanted nothing else to matter.

Through Diana, I rediscovered the meaning of true partnership. Every act of care she extended was more than just duty; it was a sign of our deep connection and unspoken understanding. The accident had robbed me of my independence, but it had also forged an unbreakable bond between us. It was right there in front of me, and I was in too much distress to appreciate her as much as I should.

As days turned into weeks, I realized how much her unwavering support meant to me. Her strength became my anchor, grounding me in moments of despair. She was no longer just my wife; she was my lifeline, my reason to keep fighting. Our relationship, which had been based on mutual independence for longer than I thought, now evolved into a symbiotic existence where each of us drew strength from the other.

I learned to appreciate the minor victories we shared—her gentle encouragement when I took a few steps, the quiet moments of connection when words weren't necessary, and the unspoken promise that we would face this challenge together. Diana's presence was one of the most paramount reasons my suffering was bearable, and her resilience gave me the courage to endure.

In Diana's unwavering presence, amid the pain and despair, I found a reason to cling to life, a reason to believe that maybe, just maybe, there was more.

Chapter Fifteen

If at any point I had been told that I wasn't alive, there's a chance I would have believed it. It would have been easy to accept that my triumph had been an illusion and my pain was the torment. The greatest agony all came from watching as my skin was scraped off. After countless weeks of this experience, the feeling had not turned into any kind of norm for my body to accept. The pain was afresh every single time, every day, until the very last, which I had almost lost hope was ever going to happen and could have any sooner.

If it had slipped out of the lips of the people who took care of me, how could I have fought it? To watch one's flesh being torn from the bone was not an experience a living person usually endured, yet that was the feeling I had with every session of the procedure.

It was one of the last days of my skin debridement, and the procedure was no less excruciating than the first day I was subjected to it. Amid the unbearable pain, there was a strange sense of joy and relief. The sense of gratitude was well within me at the realization that this agonizing and demoralizing part of my healing journey was finally nearing its end.

The nurses had assured me, "The home stretch was near," as they called it, their voices cheerful despite the grim reality it had been. The truth was far less optimistic. It had felt more like a medieval torture method. Each session left me drained, a hollow shell of my former self. Yet, today, a sliver of hope bloomed among the despair. This, I told myself, *This agonizing scrape could be the last*—a small milestone on a seemingly endless road to recovery.

I squeezed my eyes shut, forcing myself to focus on a silent prayer of thanks. The metallic tang of disinfectant stung my nostrils, a harsh counterpoint to the wave of nausea washing over me. Then the pain hit. A white-hot inferno ripped through my body, stealing my breath and leaving me trembling on the starched sheets. My barely functional knuckles turned white as I gripped the edge of the bed; the only sound was a strangled moan escaping my lips.

Again, the woman who sat near me, holding my hand as I endured it, was a constant reminder that I wasn't completely lost.

"Almost done, honey," she whispered her voice a soothing balm: her touch, a familiar anchor in this storm of pain. Then, a glint of humor flickered in her eyes, a challenge in the face of adversity.

It was soon to be over, and I was growing nearly impatient. Finally, the session was done, and I took a deep breath of relief. The regard for my triumph wasn't, however, as instant as I had expected, as I noticed the expressions on the faces of the doctors and nurses. It was the first sign that the euphoria I was feeling was fleeting, and I almost blamed myself for getting carried away.

The debridement was supposed to be one of the last, if not the very last, session, but during the procedure, it was discovered that I had developed an infection from one metal that had been embedded in me to keep me alive. It was contributing to my pain, but even more so, it could become life-threatening if not dealt with.

Like crashing from the top of a hill after taking in a view of the world, I fell face down. After weeks of escape, thinking I was near to a complete discharge, I was bundled back to the intensive care unit, where I had to wait and be prepared for the procedure. A harsh reminder that my struggle was far from over.

Diana's comfort was still persistent. She took my hand and smiled as she told me everything was going to be okay. It was hard to feel the warmth from her touch and difficult to see any good thing in the setback when I'd been returned to the ICU feeling like a reject, even though it was the circumstance that had been the culprit. The infection that could undermine everything I had gone through was discovered, and I needed urgent care to make sure it didn't get worse and I didn't die. I wasn't quickly seeing it, instead, I was clouded by frustration as Diana held on to me and said, "By the way, happy Father's Day," her voice barely a whisper.

Carmelo Rodriguez

A choked laugh escaped my lips, surprising even myself. The absurdity of the situation and the timing, the irony of celebrating fatherhood while trapped in this medical purgatory, struck a conflicting note that somehow resonated with a deep truth.

It was like when we both realized, as weird as it was, that even the word "happy" could be used, let alone that there was anything to celebrate. The shared gallows humor became a lifeline, proof of our spirit's resilience. The laugh was as strained and rough around the edges as it could be, and it was laden with the bitterness of pain that lingered from the procedure I was soon to be put through again.

The irony of not having been much of a "father" in the past months since my accident was both depressing and darkly humorous. Diana and I laughed even harder because of it. I love my kids deeply, and Diana and the kids knew that. However, being confined to the hospital for so long and barely able to do anything fatherly for them felt like a betrayal of some sort.

Seeing them only sparingly, unable to participate in their lives as I once did, weighed heavily on my heart. Nevertheless, Diana chose that moment to remind me of Father's Day, a bittersweet acknowledgment of my role. It was a moment when I felt especially conflicted, yet her humor served as a welcome distraction until it was time for my procedure.

Diana's "Happy Father's Day" might've landed a little off-key, bordering on sarcastic with the timing, but looking back, it was pure Diana - her way of reminding me through a touch of humor, who I was, even if I felt like I was failing. It was a clumsy comfort, a nudge back toward the dad I still was, even if the hospital gown felt like a costume. In hindsight, it was the perfect distraction, a reminder of why I needed to heal and overcome all medical obstacles.

***

I survived the abrupt return to the ICU. The metal was removed and replaced, and I didn't have to face another extensive period being so restricted. It was finally time to return to the "proper" recovery process, and that was where therapy came in once again.

Learning to walk again was one of the hardest things I've ever done, but my therapist, who was nine months pregnant and a hard-ass full of jokes, made it bearable. I couldn't have asked for a better person to help me through this grueling process. Her unique blend of toughness and humor was exactly what I needed. She joked that I would be the one to put her into labor, and honestly, I tried. Every morning was a back-and-forth of comical banter and positive motivation, pushing me to get my ass up because I had shit to do.

"Get your booty movin'; you got places to be!" were the kinds of things she'd boomed, her voice a beacon of motivation.

Carmelo Rodriguez

She was the perfect accomplice in this grueling quest. Her relentless encouragement was infectious. She was a powerhouse, waddling into each session with a determined gleam in her eye, making it clear that there were no excuses. Her humor was a breath of fresh air in the sterile, often somber environment of the rehabilitation center. She had a way of making the most mundane and painful exercises seem like the most important tasks in the world.

"Come on, think I'm hauling this kid around just to watch you sit pretty?" she quipped, and I couldn't help but laugh, even when it hurt. Her jokes were sometimes borderline ridiculous, but they lightened the mood and distracted me from the pain and frustration of my situation.

Every step forward was a minor victory, celebrated with high-fives and laughter. She made me believe I could do it, that I could reclaim my life. Her confidence in me was unshakeable, and that gave me the strength to push through the pain.

The rest of the therapy team was just as dedicated. They built a haven of support, encouraging and relentlessly pushing me toward recovery. They were a well-oiled machine, each member playing a crucial role in getting me back on my feet. Their collective effort was nothing short of miraculous. They didn't just see me as a patient; they saw me as a person, and they were committed to helping me reclaim my life.

BEYOND LIMITS

They seemed always to know more than I did. Every time I wanted to give up, every time I wanted to stop because my body couldn't go any further, they wouldn't let me.

All their efforts paid off, and despite my constant worries, it would happen; I was finally told that I could be discharged home for continued care. It was the best news I had heard in months. The thought of succumbing to fate's tricks and never leaving the hospital had haunted me, so the prospect of returning home filled me with more delight than I had imagined possible.

I was far from being out of the woods, but it was a significant step in the right direction. It felt like a milestone that was nothing short of a miracle. As the doctors informed Diana and me about the measures we would need to take and the nurses counseled us on the challenges ahead, I was barely bothered. I couldn't wait to escape the sterile atmosphere where I had felt trapped for what seemed like forever.

Grateful as I was to the doctors, nurses, and the rest of the medical staff who had fought to bring me back from the brink of death and guide me toward recovery, I didn't want to spend a single minute longer in the hospital than necessary. The hospital had been my lifeline, but it also became a symbol of my confinement. The endless routine of medical checks, the constant beeping of machines, and the pervasive smell of antiseptic were daily reminders of my fragile state.

Carmelo Rodriguez

Going home meant reclaiming a piece of my old life. It meant being in a familiar environment surrounded by the love and support of my family. Even though I knew the road ahead would be challenging, the idea of facing it from the comfort of my home made it seem more manageable.

The arrangements for home care were quickly made. The doctors provided detailed instructions, and the nurses patiently walked Diana and me through everything we needed to know. Despite their warnings about the difficulties we might face, my excitement overshadowed any anxiety. The thought of sleeping in my bed, hearing my children's laughter echoing through the house, and simply being outside the confines of the hospital was exhilarating.

When the day of my discharge finally arrived, it felt surreal. The medical staff, who had become like an extended family to me, were there to see me off. Their smiles and wishes were genuine, proof of the bond we had formed through my recovery journey. As I was wheeled out of the hospital, I felt a wave of gratitude mixed with anticipation for the next chapter of my life.

Returning home marked the beginning of a new phase in my recovery, and I was eager for it to begin, eager to return to my life before the accident.

Too eager.

It all descended into a complete mess so quickly. My overwhelming desire to be done with being "cared for" made me insist on doing multiple things by myself, putting me at odds with my homecare nurse and Diana. The transition hadn't been as smooth as I had imagined. Something about being in my home but still feeling incapable struck me deeply, stirring a constant sense of rebellion within me.

Then it got worse. I had multiple meltdowns throughout the day, just trying to shower or wipe my ass without help. Each attempt at independence felt like a battle I needed to win. The frustration and helplessness were unbearable. I needed to do this. I needed to be back on my feet.

The reality of my limitations clashed violently with my expectations. Simple tasks that I had taken for granted now seemed like insurmountable obstacles. My determination to regain my independence often led to tears and anger directed at those who were only trying to help. The home care nurse's gentle and professional reminders and Diana's patient reassurances felt like shackles, binding me to a state of helplessness that I desperately wanted to escape.

I had underestimated how much my physical condition had changed and overestimated my ability to deal with it because, after all, I'd seen hell before. Each failure this time was a knock on the head about my current reality, and each meltdown was a manifestation of my frustration and despair. Diana and my homecare nurse were caught in the crossfire. I was suddenly being resentful and uncooperative.

It wasn't just about performing daily tasks; it was about reclaiming my sense of self. I was convinced I needed to prove to myself that I could still do the things I once did effortlessly. It was one thing to be at the mercy of medical helpers in the hospital, but being useless in my home was a completely different feeling.

The harder I tried, the more obvious my limitations became, and the more my frustration grew. I was stuck in a cycle of wanting to be independent and being forced to confront my helplessness.

More than ever, Diana's patience and understanding were put to the test as she navigated my emotional outbursts. She knew, more than anyone, how much I wanted to reclaim my independence, but she also saw the toil it was taking on me. Her support was unwavering, even when I lashed out in frustration. She reminded me that recovery was a process and that it was okay to need help. In those moments, all I could see was my failure to be the person I once was and how it was all unfolding in my home, of all places.

Chapter Sixteen

Therapy was grueling, but I had no choice but to remain consistent. Four times a week, every week, like clockwork. The sessions were relentless, pushing my limits and testing my endurance. I was consuming more pain medication than I care to remember; each dose was a double-edged sword that dulled the pain but reminded me of my dependence.

I was told that all of this was part of the healing process and that it was all aimed toward a goal of recovery. but the toil on my body and mind was unmistakable. My muscles ached, my joints screamed, and my spirit felt battered. The evidence of my struggle became increasingly overwhelming.

For a couple of weeks, Diana had to change the sheets almost every day because I bled through everything. The wounds from my surgeries and the physical strain of therapy caused constant bleeding, staining our bed with tangible proof of my suffering. Each morning, the sight of fresh blood was a stark reminder of the battle my body was fighting. It was disheartening, to say the least, and added to my frustration and intolerance of not being dependent. I could not sleep. It wasn't long before I ended up in trauma counseling.

I'd seen things rough when I was in the military, and that had demanded some level of counseling, but ultimately, the accident was different, trauma nonetheless.

The physical therapy sessions blurred into one another in a relentless pursuit of regaining my mobility. Each day, pushing the boundaries of what I had been told was possible, a persistent fire fueled me. Every agonizing step, every conquered exercise, every movement I remastered was a brick laid on the path back to independence. I was battling it all, knowing fully well it was the least I could do after demanding to live, refusing to give up my breath, and putting my family through the hardest of times. I couldn't keep it "regular" when I owed it to myself and everyone who was invested in me to get back on my feet, and it wouldn't be long before that happened.

The glorious day arrived. Without the familiar aid of crutches or any other form of assistance, I took a tentative step. Another, the world solidifies beneath my feet like a newborn, only I wasn't some toddler. It wasn't the most graceful walk, but it was a symphony of motion, proof of the unwavering determination that had become my core despite everything. I once stared at my legs mangled without a clue if I could stand erect again; the same legs now held me strong.

BEYOND LIMITS

With newfound confidence, I turned my focus to my hands. After all those surgeries and sessions, the daunting ordeals, I ultimately came out the other end, and they became steppingstones. The day the last bit of metal was extracted, and the last stitch snipped was a victory. Therapy continued to be grueling with the constant push toward regaining not just function but a sense of purpose. Every milestone, every regained movement, chipped away at the despair, replacing it with a flicker of hope toward my physical fitness. I was finally getting there.

One afternoon, an uncontrollable urge seized me. I called for Diana, the anticipation buzzing in my veins. As she appeared on the porch, a familiar scene unfolded before me: the street where I'd once envisioned a future; I was confined to a wheelchair for so long. Today, the narrative has changed. I took a deep breath and launched myself forward. It wasn't a sprint at first, more of a determined jog, but it was movement. Tears welled in my eyes as I ran, the wind whipping past my face, carrying away the doubts and limitations that had haunted me for so long.

When I finally stopped, panting and exhilarated, my gaze met Diana's. Her face, etched with worry for so long, was now full of pure, unrestrained joy. She broke down into tears of happiness, reflecting the overwhelming emotions surging through me.

At that moment, the unspoken words echoed between us. This wasn't just my victory; it was ours. It was her unwavering support, the shared tears and laughter, the staunch belief that had carried us through the darkest hours. She was there when the doctors told me I would be lucky if I could stand on my feet again, and there was a possibility that I might never walk again, let alone run. Time had passed, and here I was, making my way up and down the street in what was a blitz compared to what we'd both imagined I was capable of.

I ran over to Diana, and we launched into each other's arms, a tangle of limbs and emotions. The journey had been arduous, a relentless battle against limitations, but as we held each other close, the immensity of what we had accomplished washed over me. We had defied the odds, reclaimed my life bit by bit, and in that shared moment of triumph, the future stretched before us, open and full of possibility.

Just like everything about man, the mind and the body sometimes move at different paces. While my physical recovery had reached a considerable milestone, I would soon find out that I had work left undone.

Besides being able to move considerably better, despite the pain being persistent, trauma counseling took a pivotal role in getting me to the next phase because everything on the entertainment side of my life had come to a halt. I had stopped writing and felt an overwhelming sense of guilt, which soon spiraled into a deep depression. Every time I got into a car, I experienced panic attacks so severe that I often had to pull over to the side of the road or call for an Uber. That phase was incredibly difficult to overcome.

BEYOND LIMITS

I was plagued by nightmares almost every night, vivid and horrifying recollections of the accident. I could smell my skin burning and relive the searing pain in my arm as it hung from my body and in my leg, which was completely deformed. I saw the bones sticking out of my arm, blood running everywhere, and the terrified faces of those who watched my life slipping away.

How am I not dead yet? I asked myself repeatedly. The nightmares made the trauma feel fresh, preventing me from moving forward. Each one was a brutal reminder of the physical and emotional scars I carried. The sheer intensity of the memories was paralyzing, keeping me trapped in a cycle of fear and despair.

My creative pursuits, which once were a source of joy and expression, felt meaningless. The guilt of surviving while still feeling so broken consumed me. I couldn't find the strength to write or engage in anything I once loved. The depression was a heavyweight, making it difficult to see a way out.

Over time, I realized that I needed help to navigate these overwhelming feelings. Therapy became a crucial part of my recovery, helping me process the trauma and heal emotionally. Gradually, I confronted my fears and worked through the guilt that had taken hold of me. The panic attacks lessened, and I slowly reclaimed parts of my life that I thought were lost forever.

I did not give up.

Even trapped in the wreckage of my current situation, a part of me, a defiant ember, refused to be extinguished. Every morning, a gruff but unwavering voice echoed in my mind: "Get your ass up. You're not done yet. People need you." The pressure to maintain a facade of strength, to embody the motivational voice I offered others, gnawed at me. Words are power, and I clung to the ones I spoke.

This internal dialogue became my armor against despair and fueled my determination to wring every ounce of effort from my weakened body. Before therapy, I forced myself into a semblance of a workout routine, the tremors in my muscles evidence of the struggle. Each session with my therapist became a battlefield, where I pushed myself to the limit, determined to honor the warrior within. Slowly, there were signs of progress. A flicker of a smile from the therapist, a hint of admiration in her eyes; these became my external validation, proof that even in the darkest moments, the embers of hope could still ignite.

I applied a similar routine to the mental part of my recovery. It was important to understand where the problem came from and to let my subconscious get the message that I had indeed survived that I was out of the woods, and, more than anything, that I absolutely deserved to be alive because I never let myself be held down by my limitations, no matter how many times they appeared or how many times fate tried to undermine my efforts.

BEYOND LIMITS

I battled the metaphorical demons that came with challenging fate and cheating death; I realized it was far from easy to pull a win when it seemed like everything could be against you, closing your eyes to the support that surrounded you. I fought myself throughout the way to get back, not only on my feet but also the mentality that had allowed me to crawl out of the dirt where I ended up so that I could be found and saved. I had to remind myself that it was no fluke. The trauma I had carried over from my experiences was the weight I had to deal with and some of them I didn't even know still lingered.

Surviving meant facing it all, pushing the wall every time it caved me in. Going through the grinders, being mangled, and having everything turned over, every part of my life tested, but coming out the other end, still standing.

Chapter Seventeen

Therapy was a marathon, not a sprint. There were days when progress felt like a mirage shimmering in the distance. But amidst the struggle, there was a beacon of motivation – the "completion of therapy" bell.

Each chime resonated through the halls, evidence of another patient's hard-won victory. Some faces were familiar, fellow travelers on this path to recovery. Others were strangers, their battles unique but with kindred determination. Witnessing their journeys, so different yet echoing my own, filled me with a mix of emotions.

Initially, I was angry that I wasn't making similar strides. This frustration, however, became a catalyst. My therapist, with her keen eye, recognized this shift. "Your turn will come," she said, a gentle nudge laced with unwavering belief, and I clung to that belief.

BEYOND LIMITS

The envy I felt transformed into fuel, propelling me forward. The final stretch became a focused sprint. Each session pushed me to my limits, a silent competition against myself. I could see the change in my therapist's eyes, a welling up that mirrored my relentless determination.

"One hundred percent" might have been a mythical summit, but the progress I'd made was undeniable. The day I walked to the bell, my body proof of the miles I'd traveled was a culmination. As I grabbed the rope, a wave of emotions washed over me—relief, pride, and a profound gratitude for the team who had guided me back to myself.

The resounding clang echoed through the room, followed by a chorus of cheers and applause. It wasn't just the end of therapy; it was the start of a new chapter, one where the echoes of that bell would forever serve as a reminder: I had conquered the toughest challenge, and I could conquer anything.

Watching myself go from being completely disabled, lying in bed, to ringing that completion-of-therapy bell was a profound journey. Now, it was time for me to go home and work on myself the best way I knew how. At this point, I didn't care about anyone's opinions or remedies on how to speed up the process. I was solely focused on my health, nutrition, and how my body felt. I was determined to get back to where I was as soon as possible.

Throughout this timeframe, I realized that pain is temporary, but to succeed, you must push past it. So, I did it every day until the exercises no longer hurt but worked. The notion that my body couldn't do something became an illusion to me. My concept was to push every boundary and limit until my goal was achieved. This mindset shift was transformative. It allowed me to see progress where others might see only struggle.

The journey wasn't just about physical recovery; it was about mental and emotional resilience. Each day presented new challenges, but I approached them with unwavering determination. I focused on rebuilding my strength, bit by bit, knowing that every effort brought me closer to reclaiming my life.

My mornings started with rigorous workouts. The exercises that once seemed impossible gradually became manageable. I listened to my body, understanding its needs and limits but always pushing just a little further. Nutrition became a key component of my recovery. I paid close attention to what I ate, fueling my body with the right nutrients to support my healing.

The day I rang that completion-of-therapy bell was a tribute to my hard work and perseverance. It was a moment of triumph, signaling not just the end of a chapter but the beginning of a new one. Returning home, I was ready to continue my journey of self-improvement with the same intensity and focus.

Today, I preach this gospel to everyone: you must push past boundaries. You must take your mind to a different place to achieve your goals because if you don't, you will be stuck. The

BEYOND LIMITS

limits we perceive are often self-imposed, and breaking through them requires mental fortitude and relentless effort.

I share my story to inspire others and show that no matter how dire the circumstances, there is always a way forward. It takes courage, discipline, and an unwavering belief in oneself. By pushing past boundaries and embracing the pain as part of the process, you can achieve incredible things.

In the end, it's about more than just physical recovery; it's about transforming your entire mindset. It's about believing in your potential and working tirelessly to realize it. My journey from being bedridden to ringing that bell is proof that, with determination and perseverance, you can overcome any obstacle and achieve your goals.

Regaining control has taken on a whole new meaning for me. It's not only about physical rehabilitation but also mental and emotional rewiring. Entertainment has always been a source of joy, and the legal field has been a path to stability for my family. Somewhere along the way, the pursuit of those goals overshadowed the very reason I chased them—my loved ones. The accident forced a pause, a chance to reevaluate everything.

Entertainment, which was once a passion, felt distant. Law enforcement, which was a chosen path for stability, became a heavy burden, and I was threatened with memories of the horrible things I saw. The core reason for all my efforts – my family – was getting lost in the shuffle. This realization struck me like a bolt of lightning. Now, with renewed purpose, I'm reclaiming my creative spark. Law enforcement remains a vital part of the equation, but focusing newfound on achieving a healthy work-life balance. The future stretches before me with the threads of passion, purpose, and, most of all, family. This journey of mine has made me realize that there's absolutely nothing I would trade for the time with the ones I care about the most.

Getting back my health has been a battle, and while I'll carry the scars – medication and potential arthritis – they won't define me. This experience has forged a different kind of strength, a resilience that fuels my determination. My goals haven't changed; they've become even more important. Rekindling my creative fire in entertainment and upholding my commitment to law enforcement, all while prioritizing precious time with family – that's the future I'm determined to create. The road might have some bumps, but my spirit is unbreakable, and I'm living life to the fullest, one step and one dream at a time.

This book isn't just a random story; it's a rebellion against limitations, a sign carved in scar tissue, and second chances. It's the story of a helmet that wasn't a barrier but a bridge – a bridge that carried me over the precipice of tragedy. Doctors painted a terrifying picture: without it, the asphalt would have become my final resting place. However, here I stand, a survivor, a living embodiment of the power of defying limitations.

BEYOND LIMITS

Drunk driving isn't a lapse in judgment; it's a loaded gun pointed at every innocent soul on the road. This book isn't about condemnation; it's about shattering illusions. It's a wake-up call for anyone who's ever considered getting behind the wheel after a drink. The consequences shatter lives and dreams. They leave families in ruins and hearts forever scarred.

This story isn't just about the scars; it's a beacon of hope that cuts through the darkness. It's a tribute to the angels in uniform – the first responders who raced to the scene, their unwavering calm amid the chaos, and the reason my heart still beats. Their bravery is a constant reminder that even in the face of limitations, humanity can rise above. They are my inspiration, proof of the boundless potential within us all.

This book is for you, the warrior facing a seemingly insurmountable battle. It's a battle cry against limitations, a roar that echoes: "Your limits do not define you!" Challenges may loom like mountains, but within you lies the strength to not only climb them but also use them as steppingstones to unimaginable heights. This isn't just a story of survival; it's a roadmap to boundless resilience. With steadfast determination, the unwavering support of loved ones, and a mindset forged in fire, you can transform obstacles into your greatest teachers. Let this book be your weapon against limitations, your fuel to push through the toughest times. You are stronger than you think, and your potential is limitless.

Carmelo Rodriguez

Let this be your reminder to grab life by the horns and live each day to the fullest, because sometimes, a second chance is all it takes to rewrite your destiny.

Most of all, let it be a reminder that limitations are not roadblocks but steppingstones. They are the very things that will make you even better, stronger, and more resilient than ever before.

You, too, dear reader, are capable of being beyond limits.

About the Author

Carmelo Rodriguez is a bestselling author, U.S. Army combat veteran, and certified life coach whose life story exemplifies resilience and transformation. Born and raised in New York City, Rodriguez experienced homelessness during his early years, a hardship that instilled in him a profound determination to overcome adversity. His journey led him to serve honorably in Iraq, where he sustained injuries that eventually resulted in a medical discharge.

Upon returning home, Rodriguez faced an unprecedented bureaucratic error: the Department of Veterans Affairs erroneously declared him deceased. This administrative mistake led to the termination of his benefits and a cascade of challenges as multiple agencies followed suit, effectively erasing his legal identity. Rodriguez's relentless battle to rectify this error and reclaim his life became the foundation of his memoir, *Dead Soldier: A Story of the Living*, which garnered national attention and highlighted systemic issues within veteran support systems.

Beyond his memoir, Rodriguez has authored over 15 books, including *Beyond Limits*. His works often draw from personal experiences, aiming to inspire and empower readers facing their challenges.

Rodriguez's academic pursuits are equally noteworthy; he holds a Bachelor of Arts in Criminal Justice, an MBA, and has completed executive education in negotiations at Harvard Business School. Currently, he is a PhD candidate specializing in strategic marketing.

In addition to his writing and academic endeavors, Rodriguez is the founder of Battle Scarr Apparel and the creator of the Vet Doc Series, platforms through which he continues to advocate for veterans and share stories of resilience.

Through his multifaceted career, Carmelo Rodriguez remains dedicated to uplifting others, using his experiences to guide those navigating trauma, identity crises, and the pursuit of purpose.

BEYOND LIMITS

Carmelo Rodriguez

www.ingramcontent.com/pod-product-compliance
Lightning Source LLC
Chambersburg PA
CBHW060352110426
42743CB00036B/2817